# CONTEMPLATIVE PARTICIPATION

## *Sacrosanctum Concilium:* Twenty-five Years Later

*Mary Collins, O.S.B.*

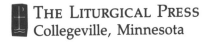

THE LITURGICAL PRESS
Collegeville, Minnesota

Cover by Don Bruno

| 1 | 2 | 3 | 4 | 5 | 6 | 7 | 8 | 9 | 10 |
|---|---|---|---|---|---|---|---|---|---|

**Library of Congress Cataloging-in-Publication Data**

Collins, Mary, 1935–
    Contemplative participation : Sacrosanctum Concilium, twenty-five years later / Mary Collins.
       p.  cm.
    Includes bibliographical references.
    ISBN 0-8146-1922-3 : $5.95
    1. Catholic Church—Liturgy.  I. Title.
BX1970.C656  1990                         90-36016
264'.02'009045—dc20                    CIP

*To my parents Homer and Lauretta,*
*who taught me to pray with confidence,*
*never to lose hope,*
*and to discern what is good.*

# Contents

# Introduction

The essays collected here were prepared for the spring 1989 lecture series at the Irish Institute for Pastoral Liturgy in Carlow. Their original audience was a group of priest and lay leaders, some from England and Scotland as well as Ireland, who have pastoral responsibility for public worship and who gather for two days each spring to pray and reflect together on the liturgical renewal of Vatican II and their own pastoral situation. The role of the invited expert is not to interpret their situation for them but rather to begin a conversation among them about the larger ecclesial and cultural context within which they are working as pastors, catechists, and teachers.

The six topics selected for the series are indicative of our larger ecclesiastical and social realities, but they make no claim to provide either an exhaustive or definitive account of the liturgical environment twenty-five years after the Vatican Council. Because each piece was conceived as a conversation starter, my aim has been to engage first hearers and now readers in thinking about familiar liturgical matters in somewhat unconventional ways. If the engagement occurs here among readers, my limited goal will have been reached. But there are many more books and articles for the diligent to take up. So I have offered some brief suggestions for further reading, confident that each source will lead the curious reader to another.

My tone in this assessment of our current situation twenty-five years after Vatican II's Constitution on the Liturgy is essentially positive, although there is plenty of ground for questioning whether all that is going forward officially in the name of the liturgical renewal is congruent with the fundamental intentions of the reform. The 1988 authorization of (what might even be seen as the Roman promotion of) the use of the preconciliar liturgical books, the so-called Tridentine liturgy, in every diocese of the universal Church has certainly introduced ambiguity and a good measure of confusion into the present situation. The 1963 reform enunciated as a key principle that the "full and active participation of all the people [in the Church's public worship] is to be considered before all else" (*Sacrosanctum Concilium* 14). It is hard to make the case that the prereform books and the underlying ecclesiology within them promote that goal.

Similarly, the 1989 Roman promulgation of a document providing for a Sunday non-Eucharistic assembly in the absence of an ordained priest works at cross purposes with the express intent of the Constitution on the Sacred Liturgy. That conciliar document could not be clearer in its affirmation that the Sunday Eucharist is the normative liturgical celebration of the Catholic people. But rather than facing the pastoral situation directly and asking what has to be done to make that norm the reality in the universal Church, the Holy See has promulgated a document once again calling the Church to adjust to the abnormal as the norm. By institutionalizing this "priestless" pastoral solution to the demands of the Sunday assembly, the Church at Rome has seemed to reject both the spirit and the letter of *Sacrosanctum Concilium,* which was directed to making the revitalization of the Sunday Eucharist the heart of the liturgical renewal.

Neither the reemergence of the preconciliar liturgy nor the normalizing of priestless Sundays is taken up here, for neither is congruent with the teaching of the Constitution on the Sacred Liturgy. These essays are directed to what is going forward in the spirit of the reform. What has begun to take root in these past twenty-five years is already giving rise to the future of Catholic worship.

# 1

## Local Church Reception
## of Conciliar Reform

Catholic communities in all parts of the world have been engaged in interacting with the new liturgical books, which were a first fruit of the Vatican II mandate for liturgical reform. This interaction is a process theologians talk about as "reception." The books have been delivered; now they are being appropriated within the local contexts in which Catholics live, work, and pray. The process of reception is a process of interpretation.

In our highly centralized Church it is commonly assumed that the work of interpretation belongs solely to those with juridical competence. The pope makes decisions, the Vatican curial offices make decisions, the bishops reinforce the decisions in their dioceses, and the priests enforce them in the parishes. The work of local dioceses and parishes is to conform to the law, in this case the normative liturgical books and the many Roman directives about how to implement them. But that common-sense viewpoint needs to be examined, for the phenomenon of the actual reception of liturgical reform is more subtle and more complex.

The decision by the bishops of the Church in council that the Church's public worship be reformed was the starting point of the reform. But no reform takes hold without the assent of the Church.

9

According to the eminent French theologian Yves Congar, the local Churches are active participants in the work of liturgical reform. Reception of the reform involves local judgment that what has been offered to a local Church through its communion with the bishop of Rome and all other bishops in communion with him is good for the life of faith of the people living in this place.

In a previous era, after the Council of Trent, those who exercised the teaching office of the Church had made the judgment that the good of the Church would best be served by leaving nothing to pastoral choice in the celebration of the liturgy. Priests understood it to be their responsibility to read the Latin liturgy as printed and to move and gesture precisely as the books prescribed. Appropriate reception of the sixteenth-century liturgical reform of the Council of Trent required no more and no less than absolute conformity to the Tridentine liturgy as it was printed in the Missal and the sacramental ritual books of Pope Pius V. Those official books were modified only in the slightest ways during the next four hundred years.

The liturgical reform of Vatican II proceeded from a different premise. The postconciliar Roman liturgical books have been so composed that they require judgment, decision, and choice. You experience the impact of those judgments, decisions, choices, when you note the differences in the Sunday liturgy as you travel in your city, in your diocese, or in other cities and dioceses across the country and across the world. In one parish the local practice at Communion reflects the fullest possible active participation of the laity: the bread of the Eucharist in the people's hands, the cup taken and shared, laymen and laywomen collaborating with the ordained priest in ministering bread and cup, the laity blessed and sent out to take Communion to the parish's homebound members. In other parishes we observe different behaviors among both the clergy and the laity, the results of different choices, judgments, decisions. In fact, local leaders are often unaware of the power they exercise when they refuse to make pastoral judgments.

How might we account for the distinct difference of viewpoint? The answer lies in developments in ecclesiology. Our Vatican II understanding of the mystery of the Church is the basis for grasping the dynamics that have controlled the reception of the liturgical reform these past twenty-five years.

This essay will focus on the matter of the reception of the Vatican II liturgical reform. First we will consider reception as a theological category developed to account for an ecclesiological phenomenon. Next we will consider the theology of the local Church as it has been evolving since Vatican II, and in this context we will identify particular liturgical assemblies as distinctive social actors in the ecclesial reception of the liturgical reform. Then we will consider from an ecclesiological point of view the self-correcting nature of the reception process.

## Reception as a Theological Category

To speak of the reception of the liturgical reform mandated by Vatican II in 1963 is to speak of the process of ecclesial assent. The bishops in solemn council voted a liturgical reform for the sake of an ecclesial renewal. But the actual fate of that reform has been dependent not simply on what the bishops did together in council but on the subsequent local appropriation—in particular dioceses and national episcopal conferences—of what the council had committed itself to doing.

Yves Congar teaches us to see reception as the process by which a local Church takes into its own life particular teachings and disciplinary norms that have risen elsewhere. When the local Church incorporates such teachings and norms it is affirming, acknowledging, attesting, that the matters being so received will be good for the Church. All such reception of teachings and norms from elsewhere into the life of the local Church inevitably involves a judgment on the worth of the teachings and norms at issue. Reception is, in principle, a selective process; the judgment of assent implies at least the possibility of an alternate decision to reject.

Two typical approaches to the theology of reception rise from two types of ecclesiology. An ecclesiology of communion will give rise to an interactive understanding of the process of reception. A hierarchical ecclesiology will give rise to a one-directional understanding of how doctrines and disciplines are to be responded to. The first approach to assent, grounded in an ecclesiology of communion, is the more ancient; the second approach to assent, based on a hierarchical and even monarchical ecclesiology, is the more familiar. We will consider the later, more familiar viewpoint first.

From this viewpoint we might think of reception as a transaction in which the "message received" in the local Churches can be expected to correspond exactly to the "message sent" from Rome. If we consider the reception of the liturgical reform in these terms, the task of evaluating the progress of the reception of the reform is quite simple. Official documentation has carefully recorded for us all of the "messages sent" to the Churches since the promulgation of *Sacrosanctum Concilium* in 1963. *Editio typica* of all the liturgical rites have been prepared, each with ritual text and theological *praenotanda*. Follow-up instructions from bodies charged with the implementation of the reform have persistently clarified matters when it became evident that there was disagreement in parts of the Church about what the reform required. Think, for instance, of the Directory for Masses with Children, of the Instruction Concerning Receiving Communion in Both Kinds, or of the Third General Instruction for the Orderly Carrying Out of the Constitution on the Sacred Liturgy.

Our evaluation of the reception of the Vatican II liturgical reform might, from this viewpoint, consist of efforts to measure the degree of conformity in the Churches with what is prescribed and proscribed by the various official documents that have appeared in the past twenty-five years. More subtlety could be introduced into this evaluation if we took note of the matters that have been most frequently emphasized in subsequent decrees and instructions to find out what the trouble spots are. It is conventional wisdom that frequent repetition of legislation is a signal that the matters attended to in the legislation are being poorly received and must be emphasized. An alternate approach to interpreting the phenomenon of recurrent instructions might suggest that the authorities are themselves selectively promoting certain doctrines and disciplinary norms according to some well-defined or ill-defined criteria of significance.

Two things typically characterize this familiar understanding of the reception process. First, it rises from an ecclesiology that clearly identifies a single ecclesiastical center. Secondly, authority resides in that ecclesiastical center for passing judgment, for evaluating what is good for all the Churches, and for requiring assent.

Despite the familiarity of the assumptions undergirding this approach to the reception of the liturgical reform, it is not the best starting point for understanding the original notion of reception. The theological concept of reception took shape when an earlier generation of theologians sought a way to interpret a curious phenomenon: that doctrines and disciplines spread from one Church to another under the ecclesiastical circumstances of the early Church. We need to consider the more ancient idea of how reception was a positive act of a local Church.

In the first millennium of the Christian Church, the basic ecclesial unit was the local or regional Church under its bishop or bishops. The universal Church was catholic precisely in its joining the many local Churches into a communion. Such local Churches held local synods in which churchmen made judgments about matters of doctrine and discipline. Now, it regularly happened that the acts of such regional synods had impact on the life of other ecclesiastical communities. Neighboring or traveling bishops recognized that disciplinary norms, ways of worshiping, and doctrinal formulations achieved in one jurisdiction might speak analogously to their own. What was judged good was assented to and appropriated.

Uniformity was not an unqualified value in this ecclesiology of communion; unity was. The Church at Rome, the center of unity, regularly resisted letting its worship be influenced by what was happening in other Churches with which it was in communion. Hence the axiom "When in Rome do as the Romans." Nevertheless, the interaction of Churches in communion with one another had an impact even on the liturgically conservative city of Rome.

In our own day, even with our dominant centrist ecclesiology, we have seen the ancient dynamics of reception at work. For example, the movement of liturgical reform and renewal that had risen in the Churches of Belgium, France, and Germany in the late nineteenth and early twentieth centuries came to Rome via a liturgical summit meeting in Assisi only in the 1950s. The movement was subsequently received by a bishop of Rome as an initiative "good for the Church"— so good, in fact, that the liturgical reform agenda was given top priority at the Second Vatican Council.

Reception as a theological category involves a process of judgment about what is good for the Church. The judgment occurs not simply by notional assent but through an actual appropriation into the Church's life of the matters it is assenting to. Both models of reception agree on that much. What they approach differently is the central locus of authority. Does authority lie at the center or in the local Churches for making judgments about what is good and for promoting assent? The alternative models are types, and as such they are helpful for analysis. But our own ecclesiastical situation is such that no simple type is functional or functioning. Our ecclesiology since Vatican II is neither an ancient ecclesiology of the communion of autonomous local Churches nor the intermediate ecclesiology of communion through a communion of patriarchs. But neither is our ecclesiology the Tridentine ecclesiology which assumes exclusive Roman hegemony. Our next concern, then, is to look at the theology of the local Church emerging since Vatican II.

## The Local Church

The phrase "local Church" has peppered this essay. It is useful now to give the term some precision. In contemporary ecclesiological discussion "local Church" is condensed speech for "the local realization of the Church in particular cultural spheres." The Catholic Church in Ireland is such a local realization of the Church in a particular cultural sphere. So also is the Catholic Church in the United States, in New Zealand, in Indonesia, in Uganda, in Scotland. It is these local Churches which at a first level are receiving or rejecting or reinterpreting the liturgical reform within their specific cultural contexts.

Postconciliar ecclesiologists note that the universal Church exists only as a communion of all such local Churches. Local realizations of the Church are not parts of some preexisting whole. Ecclesiologists direct our attention to the truth that local Churches are "local realizations of all that the Church is." They cite *Lumen Gentium* 23: "In them and out of them . . . the one and holy Catholic Church comes to exist." Local Churches come to be through "the call of God, the word of Christ, the grace of the Spirit, and the exercise of the apostolic ministry, especially through the Eucharist."

Mention of the Eucharist as a central activity by which the local Church comes to be presses us to move the discussion about local Church to an even more circumscribed frame. For of course there is no generalized Eucharistic celebration of the local diocese. There are only the particular liturgical assemblies of St. Anne's parish or St. Martha's or the particular liturgical assemblies at the cathedral. Bishops acting as the principal liturgists of their dioceses or territorial conferences of bishops may promote or reject proposed doctrinal understandings or ritual norms. But whether the doctrines and normative behaviors are brought to life in the cultural sphere is finally a judgment made by a local pastor with his parishioners. Particular liturgical assemblies author themselves to a significant degree. They bring themselves into being by the way they choose to live and worship, and in this work of constituting themselves they have authority.

An example can clarify the point. Almost immediately after the Vatican Council, the bishops of Zaire initiated a process leading to the development of an indigenous rite for a Church located in middle-belt Africa. The process involved numerous consultations among ecclesiastics and academics, Zairians and Romans, and culminated in a 1988 Roman approbation and a Zairian promulgation of the rite. But neither the Roman Congregation for Worship nor the episcopal conference can assure that the *Rite Zairois* will be received in the parishes of Kinshasa or in the churches and chapels of the bush. Nor can they be certain that where the new rite is received in particular liturgical assemblies it will be performed precisely according to the normative text and with the same intentionality as was agreed upon by the hierarchical authorities who produced the official ritual texts.

A second example can be drawn from the experience of Catholics in the United States. In the past twenty years parishioners in cities and towns across the United States have commonly celebrated the *mandatum* on Holy Thursday as a ritual celebration of the mystery of Christian service. Parish staff—clergy and laity together—have washed the feet of representative parishioners, old and young, male and female. A 1988 Roman instruction insisted that the sole authentic celebration of the *mandatum* involves the ordained pastor's washing, *in persona Christi,* the feet of twelve men, *in persona apostolicae.*

The response of local Churches to the narrowed interpretation of the *mandatum* provides some interesting data for reflection on the exercise of authority in the reception process. In one major archdiocese, with the cardinal-archbishop playing no evident directive role, the *mandatum* has been practically displaced in suburban parishes by an alternate ritual of hand washing in which every single member of the assembly participates. There are here no representatives *in persona* anybody. In other dioceses of the United States many parishes, with the tacit approval of their bishops, continue to celebrate the *mandatum* according to their established custom of twenty years, having made pastoral judgments based on local experience about what is doctrinally or ritually authentic. In still other dioceses where bishops have insisted on a strict adherence to the Roman norm for the proper celebration of the rite, local pastors in consultation with their lay liturgy teams have made judgments to suppress the rite altogether because of the discord its males-only performance would introduce into the Holy Thursday liturgy. One hapless bishop finally suppressed the rite himself during the 1989 Triduum at which he presided when he was visibly moved by the discord he had unwittingly generated by his pastoral letter to his diocese endorsing the Roman pseudoclericalized interpretation of the *mandatum*.

The narration of particular cases underscores the role the particular liturgical assembly plays in the process of the reception of the liturgical reform. Parishioners themselves in concert with or in tension with their pastors affirm that certain matters proposed for public worship are good for the Church—or they act to reject them.

Nevertheless, local liturgical assemblies and even whole local Churches can be victims of their own inauthenticity. Consequently, a theological exploration of the process of the reception of the liturgical reform cannot avoid raising questions about the soundness of the judgments being made.

## The Authenticity of Judgment in the Local Churches

The first safeguard for the promotion of an authentic reception of liturgical reform at the level of the particular liturgical assembly is appropriate leadership within the local Church. Episcopal conferences can promote liturgical catechesis; they can develop programs and establish institutes to assist the parishes to learn new patterns of liturgical behavior that the conferences judge to be potentially good for the local Church. Episcopal conferences can provide suitable resources. Yet in the final analysis it is the believing community gathered in its particular liturgical assembly, presided over by its pastor, that gives expression to the faith that is in it. It does this in the way it uses, reinterprets, and suppresses elements of the normative liturgical books.

Is there a fail-safe structure to prevent particular liturgical assemblies—the most local of all local realizations of the Church in a particular culture—from closing in on themselves? At one level the answer is no. And the data for the judgment comes from both theological and historical sources.

Historical investigation teaches us that every significant achievement in the effort to preserve the apostolic faith is always a partial achievement of the truth. It presents us with truth; it does not exhaust the mystery. In retrospect we are capable of recognizing the brilliant insights of those who have gone before us, but we can also see the distortions in their expressions of faith which were the result of blind spots in their vision. Theologically, we recall that both the local Church's self-constituting acts and the particular liturgical assembly's celebrations of the mystery of Christ take place in history. As historically contingent events, they involve freedom and risk. Every liturgical achievement will mix authentic faith and communal inauthenticity. But on another level, an ecclesiology of communion can provide a more constructive theoretical answer to the question. And attending to actual ecclesial praxis can confirm the theory.

The Catholic Church differs from sectarian groups in its adherence to the mystery of ecclesial communion. The living tradition of all the Churches is the authentic witness to the apostolic faith. So the local Churches must give an account of their faith, and they must receive the witness of the other Churches. Giving an account of their own faith requires that some in the local Church have a capacity for critical self-reflection. Receiving the witness of other Churches means being open to discovering the apostolic faith expressed in ways previously unanticipated, even unthought and unimagined. Liturgical hospitality, ecclesial communion, and self-critical reflection are essential aspects of the local Church's search for authenticity in the reception of the liturgical reform.

Again, a case may help illustrate the theoretical dynamic. During this past Easter season I celebrated Sunday Eucharist at a major pilgrimage center. At Communion the priest offered me the Eucharistic bread and said, "The Body and Blood of Christ." The proclamation startled me. The Roman liturgy offers precise formulas for the presentation of the sacramental elements in the Communion rite. His proclamation was idiosyncratic and my attention was diverted from the ritual act. What did he mean? Was it the authentic faith of the Church he was proclaiming and to which he invited my assent? His proclamation was certainly a theological declaration; he was inviting me to assent to the late medieval teaching on Eucharistic concomitance. But the occasion was liturgical and the declaration was misplaced.

Subsequently I reconstructed the process that might have led him to his proclamation. First, at no time does this particular pilgrimage center offer Communion in two kinds to the lay worshipers who gather there. In that sense it is in continuity with a past moment in the tradition when a theology of concomitance and the suppression of lay cup-sharing developed concurrently. But by maintaining continuity with this moment in the tradition, this pilgrimage center has rejected rather than received the Vatican II reform with its provision for the restoration of the cup to the laity. The pastoral staff might have had a myriad of reasons for this decision, each of which could be examined on its own merits.

Nevertheless, the idiosyncratic formula reflected some unease within the speaker. Why not simply say, "The Body of Christ," using the approved Roman Church proclamation? I wondered. Were pilgrims visiting from scattered local Churches raising questions and registering complaints about noncompliance with the General Instruction on the Roman Missal, which provides for lay Communion in two kinds? Did the staff—or this staff member only—seek theological justification for the deviant liturgical practice of the place? And having found a theological justification, did the staff—or this staff member only—determine to alter the proclamation in order to establish alternate authority for its nonreception of reformed ritual practice?

The suppression of the normative Roman liturgical proclamation and the substitution of a medieval theological formulation as an alternative proclamation has probably had the effect of bringing greater harmony and congruence into the Communion rite from the viewpoint of those who minister in that place. But from the viewpoint of a visiting worshiper I question the too-easy suppression of tension between the theological and liturgical realms. Underneath the perfunctory exchange was at least a tacit judgment that the Tridentine norm prevailed. The attitude expressed was this: While it may be possible to restore the cup to the laity it is not necessary, that is, not to the good of the Church. The Vatican II norm that restored the Eucharistic cup to the laity did so on grounds that this provided a fuller celebration of the mystery, which would contribute to the renewal of the whole Church. That norm has not compelled assent in this part of the Church.

## Interpreting Conflicts and Obstacles in the Reception Process

My account of a particular Communion proclamation carried with it a judgment. My narrative claimed that beneath the slight deviation in ritual proclamation lay a profound conflict in the understanding of the meaning of Eucharistic cup-sharing. My viewpoint was that of a ritual participant and a liturgiologist; the minister expressed the viewpoint of a cleric formed by academic theology out of touch with liturgical praxis. I am prepared to press the distinction further and to say the differing viewpoints finally reflect different experiences about the persistence or the passing of a thousand-year clerical culture. Whose full liturgical participation "counts" as "good for the Church"?

Such subtle ritual differences as the one I describe often expose unresolved ecclesial conflicts which are themselves being worked out in the course of the reception process. But local Church reception of liturgical reform can also be influenced by cultural dynamics that have their basis in the dominant secular culture. Again, an illustration is helpful to show the way in which the dominant culture in the United States has influenced the reception of the liturgical reform.

Recently I attended a conference on the current state of liturgical reform twenty-five years after *Sacrosanctum Concilium*. The conference was based on analysis of the self-assessments of some twenty-five parishes from across the country which considered themselves to have "good liturgy." Professionals wanted to know what, in this culture, makes "good liturgy" good for those who assemble Sunday after Sunday in these parishes. Liturgiologists and social scientists who analyzed the reports from the twenty-five parishes found one constant with many variations: Sunday Eucharistic liturgy is good when it provides an experience of community.

Analysts at the conference pursued the matter of what was not said in the parish reports. Were certain elements of Eucharistic faith missing or not adverted to because they lacked significance for the worshipers? To test the matter, one liturgiologist borrowed as a grid for his interpretation of the data the five aspects of the meaning of the Eucharist identified in Baptism, Eucharist, Ministry, the 1982 Faith and Order paper of the World Council of Churches. The paper, prepared as a consensus-testing statement, has been widely discussed among Roman Catholics. The BEM statement noted five agreed-upon constitutive meanings for the Christian Eucharist: thanksgiving to the

Father; anamnesis or memorial of Christ; invocation of the Spirit; the Communion of the faithful; and the meal of the kingdom. The meaning "Communion of the faithful" had clearly caught on as the pivotal meaning of the Roman Catholic liturgical reform. But this affirmation had a negative side; it was selective. The particular Churches that were openly pleased with the quality of their Sunday liturgical assemblies were not being attentive to large aspects of the living tradition of worship: gratitude, the paschal character of salvation, the Church's mission to the world, the ethical demands of sharing in the eschatological banquet. A large part of the Eucharistic mystery seemed to have grown dormant. Why?

A sociologist suggested that the heightened consciousness of the meaning "the Communion of the faithful" might well commend itself to late-twentieth-century worshipers as a central good because our mass society is suffering the breakdown of other major institutions of social cohesion. Analogously, it is possible to understand how the "memorial of Christ," interpreted through a specific understanding of the category of sacrifice, could have been "good for the Church" in other cultural epochs. For medieval Christians "sacrifice" had become so helpful to the Church's self-understanding that the meaning "sacrifice" had displaced virtually all other Eucharistic signification—including the meaning "the Communion of the faithful."

It was not hard to achieve group consensus during the conference on the power of the contemporary cultural bias in favor of interpreting Eucharist as meaning "community." But the perception of cultural bias raised further questions. Liturgy celebrated as "good for us" in a particular liturgical assembly within a particular local Church is not necessarily effective "for the life of the world." A particular field of meaning within the complex symbol of Christian Eucharist will always be the point of engagement for each local realization of the Church in its particular cultural sphere. But the point of entry—what is heard immediately as "good news"—cannot be the final resting place for the local Churches.

## Summary and Conclusions

The many aspects of the Eucharistic mystery need to be celebrated together in our liturgical assemblies in ways that heighten rather than eliminate evangelical tension. For the reign of God which summons us transcends all the achievements of every culture. The mystery of ecclesial communion is the first reason for hope that the localized reception process can be fruitful for the renewal of the Churches. We are searching together, each in our own cultural spheres, for the way to worship the living God in spirit and in truth. Our reception of the recently revised Roman liturgical books is the concrete means given to us for this growth in faith and in prayer.

The practice of Eucharistic hospitality extended among the local Churches is a second reason for hope. Eucharistic hospitality will require that the local Churches be prepared to give an account to one another of the faith that they celebrate in their liturgical assemblies. Such witness among the many local Churches that make up the one Catholic Church will stretch each of the Churches in its capacity for self-awareness and self-criticism.

Finally, our growing capacity for ecclesial self-transcendence is a third basis for our confidence in the localized reception process. The Spirit speaks to the local Churches through their speech to one another. For example, we cannot in good conscience suppress in our celebration the ethical demands of the Eucharist when the Churches of the world's poor call us to communion with them. Nor can we ignore long the movements of the Spirit through the Church if we solemnly, ritually invoke the presence of the Spirit to bring us to the fullness of our redemption in Christ.

The many local cultural realizations of the Church beyond the city of Rome and the distinctive cultural realization of the Church that is embodied in Vatican City are each empowered through this reception process to call all others to greater authenticity. This is an aspect of the mystery within which we live, by God's grace, twenty-five years after Vatican II.

## *Suggestions for Further Reading*

*Documents on the Liturgy 1963–79*. Collegeville: The Liturgical Press, 1982. Contains translations of the major postconciliar documents. *Origins* and the Bishops' Committee on the Liturgy *Newsletter* are a source for translations of more recent and current documents from the Apostolic See and from the National Conference of Catholic Bishops.

Komonchak, J.A., ed. *The Reception of Vatican II*. Washington: The Catholic University of America Press, 1988. Translation of a collection of essays on the theological concept and the process of reception of the Council, first published in Italian as part of the assessment of twenty-five years of postconciliar developments.

Megivern, James. *Concomitance and Communion: A Study in Eucharistic Doctrine and Practice*. New York: Herder and Herder, 1963. A preconciliar study in which the author reviews the sequence of historical and theological events that led to the suppression of the Eucharistic cup for the laity in the West; it contributes to an understanding of the significance of the restoration of the cup at Vatican II.

# 2

---

# *Women in the Liturgical Assembly*

Most of us never thought about it one way or another. Or if we reflected, we thought about how reassuring it was to go to morning Mass and evening devotions and to find the church peopled with women, mostly older women. These reliable women regularly out-numbered the reliable men in the gatherings. The women were often widows, or perhaps mothers—like mine—who got up before the family, walked to the church for the 6 A.M. Mass, and were back to pre-pare breakfast for everyone. These women were strong in faith and prayer. Some prayed the Rosary; others had the *Key of Heaven* prayer book. My own mother had a St. Andrew's English-Latin Missal by 1940, and she prayed the Mass prayers themselves. Had you asked women at early-morning Mass whether they participated fully, they would have told you yes. Had you asked them if the Church discrimi-nated against them as women, they would have been puzzled by the question. When they found out what you were driving at, they would have said a clear no.

## Norms for Women's Liturgical Participation

That was before 1960. In the 1960s social changes and changes in the Church began to cause the ground to shift under us all. One seismic disruption came in the form of the event we call Vatican II, the Ecumenical Council that met from 1962 to 1965. Nothing has been the same since for Catholics, especially for Catholic women. It started innocently enough. The nearly unanimous vote on the Constitution on the Sacred Liturgy called for the reform of all the rites in order to help the Church understand more fully the mystery of Christ in which we participate and to encourage the full, conscious, and active participation of the laity in the liturgical rites themselves. The diversity of liturgical roles was to be promoted, with the laity doing all that was rightly theirs as the baptized.

Initially attention was on shifts of language from liturgical Latin to our own spoken tongues, on the priest facing the people, on the exchange of peace, on adjusting to new times for kneeling and standing, and on the presence of lay lectors. These were small aftershocks that sent uneven tremors through rectories and parish Churches throughout the 1970s as the new liturgy was being learned.

One tremor caused no greater or lesser adjustment than any of the others at first, as we tried to keep our balance. The 1975 redaction of the General Instruction on the Roman Missal provided the following directive for bishops:

> Laymen . . . may perform all the functions below those reserved to deacons. At the discretion of the rector of the church, women may be appointed to ministries that are performed outside the sanctuary.
>
> The conference of bishops may permit qualified women to proclaim the readings before the gospel and to announce the intentions of the general intercessions. The conference may also more precisely designate a suitable place for women to proclaim the word of God in the liturgical assembly (GIRM 70).

The appropriateness of these gender distinctions was taken for granted. In *Liturgiae Instaurationes,* the 1970 Third General Instruction on the Proper Implementation of the Liturgical Constitution, a compendium of restrictions on women's liturgical participation had been published. In summary they specified that "in conformity with norms traditional in the Church, women (single, married, religious), whether in churches, homes, convents, schools, or institutions for women, are barred from serving the priest at the altar."

Then the instructions said what baptized women might do:

> "According to the norms established for these matters, however, women are allowed to:
> a. proclaim the readings, except the gospel. . . . The conferences of bishops are to give specific directions on the place best suited for women to read the word of God in the liturgical assembly.

b. announce the intentions in the general intercessions;

c. lead the liturgical assembly in the singing and play the organ and other instruments;

d. read the commentary assisting the people toward a better understanding of the rite;

e. attend to other functions, customarily filled by women in other settings, as a service to the congregation, for example, ushering, organizing processions, taking up the collection" (*LI* 7).

These explicit declarations of gender-based distinctions in liturgical ministries, set out as self-evident, implanted an irritant in the ecclesial body. In some places the irritant was immediately painful; in other places festering began more slowly.

With the United States already caught up in the women's rights and women's liberation movements, the Catholic bishops responded promptly, trying to sooth the irritation with pastoral balm. In 1971 they made a common judgment about normative pastoral practice (see "Appendix to the General Instruction for Diocese of the United States," Sacramentary) that included the following points:

1. The reservation of a single place for all biblical readings is more significant than the person of the reader, ordained or lay; accordingly women who read should read from the ambo or lectern where the other readings are proclaimed. That is, the sanctuary is a suitable place for women readers.

2. All other ministries performed by women, such as leading the singing, are to be done in the most convenient place, whether inside or outside the sanctuary.

3. Women may not serve directly at the altar within the sanctuary.

4. Decisions about women's actual assignment to liturgical ministries will be left to the pastor in the light of the culture and mentality of the congregation.

The pastoral response was judged wise and fair by all but those few whose critical consciousness was already attuned to social reality and its assumptions about women's inferiority. The few asked questions and the questioning began to spread. The rest of this presentation will address both the pastoral developments and the feminist theological reflections that have accompanied them. In the technical language of theologians, we are reporting on praxis-based theological development. The Church is engaged weekly in acts of worship, and it is reflecting back on the significance of its ritual action. It is correlating its action with the Church's authentic tradition and with its own experience of authentic human existence.

## Liturgical Praxis

Adult women now appear regularly in the sanctuary in Catholic churches. They do all the things listed as permissible in 1970. But they do more. They enter the sanctuary to present the gifts of bread and wine; they place the gifts directly on the altar table; they set the altar table with the cloth and the sacred vessels. Women assist in the breaking of the bread and the distribution of Communion, ministering both the Eucharistic bread and the Communion cup. Then they extend their liturgical ministries from the table, bearing the Eucharist to sick and elderly parishioners in their homes.

Nor is this the limit. Women pastoral associates sit in the presider's chair in some Sunday assemblies that do not have ordained pastors. In such assemblies, by episcopal charge women read the Gospel and preach the homily. They lead the community in formal prayer. Standing at the altar table, they invite the people to Eucharistic communion in the reserved sacrament. They confer blessings. They preside in the sanctuary at wakes and funerals. The account of women's emerging roles in the liturgical assembly could go on, for it continues to grow in response to pastoral circumstances.

As the Church has become increasingly familiar with the presence of adult women in the sanctuary, first at the ambo, then at the presider's chair and at the altar table, young girls have begun to appear in the sanctuary in emulation of their mothers. They are seated alongside young boys, dressed in the alb of the acolyte. Young girls carry candles and the processional cross. They handle the thurible and incense the assembly as their brothers do. They hold the Sacramentary while the presider prays with outstretched arms. Sometimes they hand cruets to the presiding priest preparing the cup of offering.

All of this happened slowly, unevenly, within Sunday assemblies. Some places know none of it even in 1990; others have seen it all. What does it mean that these things are happening? Clearly, our practice goes beyond our normative disciplinary language. The words on the books specify that women may still be denied access to the sanctuary on the personal judgment of an individual pastor. Normative liturgical discipline stipulates that women may not read the Gospel nor give a liturgical homily. Most emphatically, women may not serve directly at the altar. But what we say officially is not really the case. The discrepancy between our words and our deeds ought to puzzle us. Is our emerging practice as a Church inauthentic, deviant, disobedient to the will of God, reprehensible? Or are these authentic developments? And how shall we know? The situation contains an imperative for us: The Church must reflect critically both on our contemporary experience, which is hospitable to adult women's unrestricted lay ministries in the liturgical assembly, and on our normative liturgical tradition, which to this day mandates gender-based distinctions in the liturgical assembly.

## Feminist Theology and Liturgical Praxis

Some of that critical reflection has already begun. Feminist theologians—notably but not exclusively Elizabeth Schüssler Fiorenza and Rosemary Radford Ruether, Marjorie Proctor-Smith and Sandra Schneiders—have been providing us with language that helps to heighten our critical awareness. They supply categories that take account of the gap between what we have been taught about women's place and our actual experience of women in the liturgical assembly. We need such technical language—words to wrap around our experiences—because we are at a historic moment. The way of our believing and the way of our praying are mutually interpreting one another, a dynamism captured in the liturgical axiom *lex orandi lex credendi*. But that is not the whole of it. For the way of our believing and the way of our praying are both also being reinterpreted by women's new readiness to claim and to proclaim their full personhood, whatever the traditions to the contrary.

Catholic feminists take it as axiomatic that the full humanity of women is integral to every authentic interpretation of the Christian message. So Catholic feminist theologians are prepared to judge as evangelically inauthentic any practice, any doctrinal formulation, any theological interpretation, any disciplinary norm, that negates the full humanity of women. The authentic gospel tradition, they assert, is whatever proclaims the full humanity of women and men and promotes the emancipation of women from inauthentic constraints on their personhood.

The implications of this norm for the liturgical tradition might not be immediately evident. For liturgy functions as a system of symbols, and in any symbol system values, ideas, and relationships are expressed in many ways. Only a small part of the meaning which public ritual bears is expressed discursively, in statements. In ritual activity the cognitive content, or meaning, is carried through one or more of many nonverbal codes. The spatial code is the most obvious of these, once we are alerted to it. Ritual space is regularly divided into zones. A typical medieval church had zones designated as sanctuary, choir, nave, narthex, and baptistry. Most of these were contiguous but distinguished by distinct elevations, gates, and screens. The baptistry was regularly set apart. Such zones are ordered to designate relative status within a group, and access to zones and movement within ritual space is a way of expressing symbolically a sense of divinely designed sacral order. With that awareness, the student of ritual can legitimately ask what is being asserted symbolically about the personhood of women through a liturgical system that denies women all access to the altar within the sanctuary?

What is notable here is that the liturgical experience of the Church these past twenty-five years bears out the feminist theologian's assertion that authentic interpretations of the Christian message involves the emancipation of women. Special restrictions on women's liturgical service in the sanctuary are increasingly being recognized as arbitrary and inauthentic because the restrictions are not grounded in the demands of Christian celebration of the mystery of Christ. Nor are such limits an expression of the actual human limits of adult females. Just the contrary is being widely demonstrated. Only the most intransigent among us continue to assert the contrary despite the evidence of cumulative ecclesial experience.

But our desire for understanding and for truth needs to be honored. Can the Church have been wrong about women's human identity in its control of women's engagement in the mystery of Christ? People rightly ask about the legitimacy and authority of magisterial teachings that say women have a "special nature" which requires that they occupy a special "women's place" in the Church, symbolized by their restricted access to significant zones in the liturgical assembly. Where are answers to be found?

*Suspicion and the Search for Authenticity.* New insights drawn from feminist biblical interpretation and feminist theology can be brought to bear on the liturgical tradition. A feminist liturgical hermeneutic, that is, a feminist approach to thinking critically about the Church's liturgical tradition, approaches the liturgical tradition with the suspicion that all liturgical forms, all ritual symbols, all texts for prayer and proclamation, all spatial arrangements, are androcentric. (The Greek word for the male human person, *aner, andros,* provides the root for this useful neologism.) Feminist thinking does not presume the liturgical tradition is innocent of such bias until proven guilty. It presumes that the bias is pervasive, because all ecclesiastical institutions have been shaped unreflectively and uncritically by male leaders who assumed male superiority and female inferiority.

Feminist interpretations of Church history take note of the fact that the world in which the Church took shape in history was androcentric and that its structures of authority were hierarchical and patriarchal. Church buildings and the norms governing the use of ritual space embodied our male leaders' perceptions of good order. And the ritual spaces they built gave credibility and authority to their perceptions. Women, controlled within ritual space, learned their place in the divine scheme of things. But we now live in a post-Copernican world and all centrisms have come under challenge: The earth is not the center of the universe; neither Europe nor North America are the center of the earth; males are not the center of the human race. So when Catholic feminists read that all women, in conformity with norms traditional in the Church are barred from serving the priest at the altar, they judge the norm, however traditional and understandably androcentric and patriarchal, to be fallacious and no longer binding. They similarly judge that the denial of women's full liturgical participation is not the authentic interpretation of the gospel of Jesus Christ.

*Authentic Ritual Proclamation.* Yet even as feminist theologians are suspicious about the androcentric bias pervading the liturgical tradition, they remain alert for emancipatory elements. They are confident that such freeing elements are present because they believe that the truth of the gospel cannot have been totally suppressed by witting or unwitting androcentrism. The Holy Spirit of Jesus remains within the Church.

Suspicion of androcentrism and patriarchal bias is only the first of several feminist principles of interpretation that can free the Church to look critically at its liturgical tradition. The second is the principle of authentic proclamation that the Church is a discipleship of equals. From a liturgical viewpoint this authentic proclamation is not simply a matter of words. It is a matter of ritual doing. The Church is already venturing such proclamation whenever the barriers keeping women out of the sanctuary are set aside. The Church is venturing the proclamation of women's full personhood whenever laywomen, like laymen, young girls like young boys, move freely and confidently within the sanctuary as ministers of worship. This authentic ritual proclamation of the Christian message has an important secondary effect. It denies the legitimacy of all earlier inauthentic ritual proclamations restricting women in the Church, even when these have appropriated the authority of unalterable divine revelation.

*Authentic Remembrance of the Tradition.* Authentic proclamation of the Christian message about men and women's equal participation in the mystery of Christ requires authentic memory. So authentic remembrance is a third feminist principle for critical interpretation of our liturgical tradition. Remembering and interpreting are inevitably selective activities. We select which in a series of episodes is significant according to some conscious or unconscious criteria of significance. And when we record what we think significant from the particular viewpoint of the community or subgroup in which we live or for whom we speak, we call that writing history.

Feminists, having learned the rules of this public craft of writing history, have committed themselves to retelling the story of the ministry of Jesus and the life of the Church by taking the viewpoint of Christian women whose voices and deeds were deemed insignificant in the first telling. They work from clues, vestiges, fragments, to trace women's active and coequal participation in the life of the Church from the apostolic generation to the present one. Like archeologists, feminist historians build from shards, aware that whole cultures can be reconstructed from very little data. Like archeologists, they lament how much has been lost by wanton destruction.

Feminists have learned to be vigilant about subtle ways in which the tradition has destroyed and continues to destroy the memory of women. How ironic it is, for example, that this postconciliar generation, which thinks of itself as having heightened sensitivity to women in the liturgical assembly, is the first generation of Roman Catholics for whom the names of the women in the ancient Roman canon are not being sounded! How seldom we hear proclaimed on Sunday the names of "Felicity, Perpetua, Agatha, Lucy, Agnes, Cecilia, and Anastasia" as those in whose company we make Eucharist! The rubric that allows for the abbreviation of the commemorations for pastoral reasons brackets out some of the men but all of the women, and many presiders consistently use the option to abbreviate, oblivious to what is going unsaid.

Authentic remembrance of the tradition requires reclaiming and proclaiming in the liturgical assembly the names of Christian women who served Jesus and who shared with Peter and Paul the apostolic charge to "those who were his own." But it also means taking note of the pervasive exclusion of Christian women from the tradition of significance; it means remembering the suppression of women's gifts and the shameful denial or distortion of women's contributions even in the shaping of the calendar of feasts and solemnities.

To consider the revelatory power of authentic remembering in the liturgical assembly, imagine adding one brief scriptural text to the liturgy of Christmas Eve in your local church, a day on which the liturgy proclaims the genealogy of Jesus. The text offered here is from the Women's Liturgy Group of New York, compiled by Ann Patrick Ware. It has been reconstructed, in these last years of the twentieth century of the Christian Era, like the Matthaean Gospel genealogy, from fragments gathered from the Old Testament. No canonical author in the formative years of the Scripture had judged it significant to remember the women. This genealogy is not copyrighted; it can therefore be used by any reader without further authorization.

> A genealogy of Jesus Christ, the son of Miriam, the daughter of Anna:
> Sarah was the mother of Isaac,
> And Rebekah was the mother of Jacob,
> Leah was the mother of Judah,
> Tamar was the mother of Perez.
> The names of the mothers of Hezron, Ram, Amminadab, Nahshon and
>      Salmon have been lost.
> Rahab was the mother of Booz, and Ruth was the mother of Obed.

Obed's wife, whose name is unknown, bore Jesse.
The wife of Jesse was the mother of David.
Bathsheba was the mother of Solomon,
Na'amah, the Ammonitess, was the mother of Rehoboam.
Ma'acah was the mother of Abijah and Asa.
Azubah was the mother of Jehosaphat.
The name of Jehoram's mother is unknown.
Athalia was the mother of Ahaziah,
Zibia of Beersheba, the mother of Jehoash.
Jecoliah of Jerusalem bore Uzziah,
Jerushah bore Jotham; Ahaz's mother is unknown.
Abijah was the mother of Hezekiah,
Hephzibah was the mother of Manasses,
Meshullemeth was the mother of Amon,
Jedidah was the mother of Josiah.
Zebidah was the mother of Jehoiakim, Nehushta was the mother of
    Jehoiakin,
Hamutal was the mother of Zedekiah.
Then the deportation to Babylon took place.
After the deportation to Babylon
the names of the mothers go unrecorded.
These are their sons:
Jechoniah, Shealtiel, Zerubbabel,
Abiud, Eliakim, Azor and Zadok,
Achim, Eliud, Eleazar,
Matthan, Jacob, and Joseph, the husband of Miriam.
Of her was born Jesus who is called Christ.
The sum of generations is therefore: fourteen from Sarah to David's
mother; fourteen from Bathsheba to the Babylonian deportation; and
fourteen from the Babylonian deportation to Miriam, the mother of
Christ.*

By imagining the annual proclamation within local Churches of this
part of the story of salvation, we can grasp something of the significance
for liturgy of the principle of authentic remembrance.

*Creative Actualization in the Liturgical Tradition.* The example just
cited actually introduces us to a fourth feminist principle for authen-

---

*Women's Liturgy Group of New York, as compiled by Ann Patrick Ware,
100 LaSalle St., New York, NY 10027. This text may be used or republished
by any reader without further authorization from any party.

tic interpretation that has bearing on our critical interpretation of the Catholic liturgical tradition. Authentic interpretation may also come through creative actualization. Through creative actualization we bring into the liturgical assembly authentic elements of the Christian tradition which have not heretofore been accorded a place in the Church's worship because of its previously unexamined androcentric bias.

Creative actualization of the tradition is most effective when the truth is not simply spoken about but embodied. We communicate ritually through our bodies. Where we have already eliminated the altar railing as a spatial barrier between the laity and the clergy, so that our bodies share an unbroken space, the local Church has made real the truth that what we have in common, our baptism in Christ, is more significant for authentic worship than what distinguishes and divides us. That same truth is effectively actualized when laity take the Eucharist into their own hands at Communion. By touching the sacrament of the Body and Blood of Christ we discover immediately that we have hands and bodies made holy and worthy by baptism. Special anointings of priests' hands only confirm what is already the case.

Similarly, women's capacity for teaching and preaching and presiding and leading the Church in prayer is being effectively established not by theological debates about women's nature and role but rather by women's actual standing before the assembly and presiding, by their standing at the ambo and reading the Word of God, by their standing beside the priest breaking the bread at the fraction rite. Concrete liturgical praxis, the Church's actual experience of women's capacity for public spiritual leadership, negates the inauthentic tradition that says women are destined by nature for passive, distinctly feminine roles. Creative actualization of an authentic liturgical tradition is the most powerful antidote to inauthenticity in all earlier achievements of the tradition.

### Summary and Conclusions

I have not spoken directly about women's ordination, nor about inclusive language. I have spoken rather about promoting the full and authentic participation of laywomen that is presently possible in a Church that still restricts ordination to males. And secondly, I have reported on the way in which feminist principles of interpretation can help us to engage in critical reflection on our tradition. It should be clear that both pastoral praxis and critical reflection are leading inevitably to an examination of the legitimacy and authority of the gender-based exclusion of Christian women from pastoral office and the liturgical leadership that office entails. That full examination is probably an event for the twenty-first century of the Christian Church, just a decade away. What we are learning right now in our liturgical assemblies is preparing us for fundamental development within the Church's tradition of public worship.

The Church in its liturgical assemblies, especially in its Sunday Eucharist, is engaged in ritual self-interpretation even as it worships the living God. Karl Rahner teaches us that all authentic self-interpretation is interpretation of our transcendental experience. In a liturgical context we might say that all authentic self-interpretation is interpretation of our participation in the mystery of Christ. Rahner also reminds us that self-interpretation takes place in history. The Church's historical effort to embody and to celebrate sacramentally the mystery of Christ involves human freedom, risk, hope, reaching out to the future, and so, the possibility of failure. Yet as Rahner notes, it is our faith that God has taken the risk of entering human history in order to reconcile the world and make all things one.

We should not be surprised that our present historical achievement in the liturgical expression of the mystery of Christ is less than perfect precisely because the tradition took an androcentric and patriarchal shape in its formative period. But neither should we fail to recognize that Catholic women's newly achieved capacity for critical awareness is grace for the Church. Recognition of inauthenticity involves a call to conversion from all that is not God. The God of history smashes idols but offers us icons of the mystery of redemption. As a Church newly open and committed to the full, conscious, and active participation of all the baptized—women and men—we are learning to see the difference between the idols and the icons.

## Suggestions for Further Reading

Carr, Anne. *Transforming Grace. Christian Tradition and Women's Experience.* San Francisco: Harper & Row, 1988. A systematic survey of the Catholic theological tradition, subjecting it to a constructive critique and proposing directions for further development through attention to the data provided by the experiences of baptized women.

Collins, Mary. "Inclusive Language: A Cultural and Theological Question," *Worship: Renewal to Practice*. Washington: The Pastoral Press, 1987. Surveys the background for and the implications of the rising concern for the use of inclusive language in the Church's public prayer.

_____. "The Refusal of Women in Clerical Circles." *Women in the Church* I, ed. Madonna Kolbenschlag. Washington: The Pastoral Press, 1987. Considers the process and the promotion of clericalization in the Church as the context for its continuing structural and theological bias against its women members. Originally an address at a conference on women in the Church.

Proctor-Smith, Marjorie. "Liturgical Anamnesis and Women's Memory: 'Something Missing.' " *Worship* 61, no. 5 (September 1987) 405–24. An analysis of Christian liturgy vis-à-vis its traditional neglect of the memory of women in its celebration of the mystery of Christ, with constructive proposals for redressing the resultant distortions in the tradition of public prayer.

# 3

## Liturgy: Corporate Public Prayer

What have we learned during the past twenty-five years of liturgical renewal in the Roman Catholic Church? In her narrative reflection *Teaching a Stone to Talk* Pulitzer Prize nonfiction writer Annie Dillard offers a deceptively simple judgment on the cumulative meanings of our recent liturgical experiences: "It is all right—believe it or not—to be people." The judgment comes during an extended reflection on her actual experiences as someone newly come to the Catholic Church in the United States in the postconciliar period. The passage which lead to the judgment begins:

> It is the second Sunday in Advent. For a year I have been attending Mass at this Catholic church. Every Sunday for a year I have run away from home and joined the circus as a dancing bear. We dancing bears have dressed ourselves in buttoned clothes; we mince around the rings on two feet. Today we were restless; we kept dropping onto our forepaws.

Then she describes some of the liturgical awkwardness in which she participated:

> No one, least of all the organist, could find the opening hymn. Then no one knew it. Then no one could sing it anyway.
>
> There was no sermon, only announcements.
>
> The priest proudly introduced the rascally acolyte who was going to light the two Advent candles. As we all could plainly see, the rascally acolyte had already lighted them.

The cataloging of awkwardness goes on at some length. But Dillard does not conclude as some (too many) have that the awkwardness means the mystery has gone out of Catholic worship. Her contemplative eye brings her to see the revelation of divine graciousness occurring in her presence:

> A high school stage play is more polished than this service we have been rehearsing since the year one. In two thousand years, we have not worked out the kinks. We positively glorify them. Week after week we witness the same miracle: that God is so mighty he can stifle his own laughter. Week after week, we witness the same miracle: that God, for reasons unfathomable, refrains from blowing our dancing bear act to smithereens. Week after week Christ washes the disciples' dirty feet, handles their very toes, and repeats, It is all right—believe it or not—to be people.
> Who can believe it?*

What Annie Dillard names with affection "our dancing bear act" I will identify here as corporate public prayer—a body of bodies at prayer. What will inform my exploration of liturgy as corporate public prayer is theory drawn from a range of cultural anthropologists, among them Clifford Geertz, Mary Douglas, Victor Turner, and Ronald Grimes. My borrowings are unashamed, even full of gratitude. But I have so appropriated the theories of others in my own work these past fifteen years that what I have to say is distinctively my own. No one of them would be required to defend my interpretations of the bearing of ritual theory on Catholic liturgy.

Ritual theory has provided us with a fresh set of usable intellectual tools we can take up to help us understand the mystery we celebrate. For it is a quite particular form of human behavior—corporate public ritual—which mediates the mystery of our salvation. "It is all right to be people." So goes Annie Dillard's reading of our awkward, unpolished liturgical performances which we Christians have never gotten quite right in two thousand years. The patristic and Scholastic adage made the same point in different language: *Sacramentum ad hominem*. Sacramental activity, symbolic behavior, is not something God

---

*Excerpts from *Teaching a Stone to Talk* (New York: Harper & Row, Publishers, Inc., 1982). Copyright © 1982 by Annie Dillard.

needs. It is something humans do precisely because we are human
and need to give flesh and bones to our prayer.

## A Working Definition

Corporate public ritual may be described as *an assembly of people
who, when it is timely, engage in patterned behavior valued as good for the
group because it confirms group identity and advances group goals.* In my
judgment this description is sufficiently comprehensive to apply to
every rite of the reformed Roman liturgy and sufficiently flexible to
allow for a fully theological interpretation of the ritual behavior being described. Yet I have a decided preference for beginning the discussion of our current experience of liturgical celebrations by using
nontheological language. Our theological categories have been worn
so smooth by use that they have no rough edges or hooks left on them
to catch our attention. We forget that our ancestors in the theological enterprise began by using ordinary language metaphorically—words
like *sacramentum,* the soldier's oath—to talk about the ineffable. But
Dillard's choice of metaphor, "our dancing bear act," may be too
rich and lively to have much theological future. We will settle for more
prosaic speech. But our attention is on the mystery present in the apparently mundane.

## The Elements of Corporate Public Ritual

*An assembly.* One of the characteristics of the liturgical reform set
in motion with the 1963 Constitution, *Sacrosanctum Concilium,* is its
effort to relocate the center of gravity in our worship through a revaluation of the liturgical assembly (7, 14). The revaluation was prepared
for in the preconciliar period by the sustained effort of the French
liturgists George Aimee Martimort and Thierry Maertens to research
the significance of the biblical concept *qahal YHWH* and its development in the New Testament as the *ekklesía toü theoü,* to show how
this biblical category shed light on the structure, content, and purpose of the liturgical assembly in the early Church and most impor-
tantly, to give an account of the medieval Church's devaluation of
the liturgical assembly.

*Sacrosanctum Concilium* bears the marks of these scholars' influence,
as does the General Instruction on the Roman Missal. In the first we
read that "liturgical services are not private functions, but are celebra-

tions of the Church . . . a holy people united and organized under
their bishop" (26). And in the 1969 GIRM we hear, "The Lord's
Supper or Mass gathers together the people of God, with a priest
presiding to celebrate the memorial of the Lord or eucharistic sacrifice." Further, we are told in the General Instruction, "Christ is really
present in the assembly itself"(7). Put simply, the liturgy engages "an
assembly of people, when it is timely."

*When it is timely.* Timeliness is the second element in my working
description of the Church's liturgy. Corporate public assemblies take
place according to established public rhythms. They are inconceiv-
able on any other terms. A people committed to public assembly must
know the days, seasons, and hours that will lay claim upon them. For
Christians, these include the Easter season and Advent, the Lord's
Day, and the middle of the night at Pascha and Christmas. In addition corporate public assemblies must take place according to established social rhythms: Newcomers to the community need to be
initiated gradually, the estranged need reconciliation; the ill, healing;
the dead, to be buried; candidates for office, to be ordained.

The timeliness of ritual assembling alerts people to the mysteri-
ous presence of abiding grace. T. S. Eliot's words in "The Dry Sal-
vages" come to mind as we try to understand how something as
uneventful as the chronological or the calendrical—ordinary time—
can mediate the presence of salvation. Yet it is through the experiences
of our faithful periodic assembling over a lifetime that we recognize that

> . . . to apprehend
> The point of intersection of the timeless
> With time, is an occupation for the saint—
> For most of us, there is only the unattended
> Moment , . . .

We assemble when it is timely; our assembling makes ordinary time
epiphany. Every seventh day becomes once again the first day, the
Day of the Lord, because we so intend it with our deed of assembling.

*Patterned Behavior.* If the times for people's assembling are not arbitrary, neither is the activity of the gathered assembly random. On
the contrary, corporate public rituals require sequenced, patterned behavior. Assemblies have work to accomplish before they can be dis-
missed, their participants dispersed. The work is repetitive. It can be

boring for those who are not genuinely engaged, but it is energizing and enlivening for those invested in the work.

Repetitive work is not inherently boring. We know how dedicated athletes are caught up—mind, emotion, and body—in the flow of the game, so that the game seems to play itself through them. The game without the players is no more than an agreed upon set of transactions and interactions. It is the players lending themselves to the game week after week who give the game its existence, even as the demands of the game give shape to the players' lives.

The players in the liturgy are the whole assembly of baptized believers. In the past twenty-five years the theological dictum that sacraments are acts of the Church has come to be understood not as an abstract principle but as a factual statement about the ritual behavior of the people of St. Mary's, St. Joseph's, St. Anne's. It is our ritual behavior as an assembled people that anthropological theory has helped us to understand. But that theoretical insight into our liturgy as fully human activity has not come at the expense of theological insight. Rather, it has helped us to appreciate in a new way how such genuinely human activity mediates divine grace. Four aspects of this pattern behavior need to be considered in turn.

1. *Symbolic behavior:* Corporate public ritual is symbolic action. Commenting on the significance of symbolic activity, the philosopher Suzanne Langer observes that "the human mind is a great transformer." Just as an electrical transformer converts energy from one form to another which is more accessible and useful, so humans signify intangible power, meaning, and aspiration through reference to tangible forms which can be seen, held, heard, felt. Corporate public ritual is always about more than immediately meets the eye.

In the city of Bologna in the industrial north of Italy in the summer of 1989, three other Sunday-morning tourists and I walked into a neighborhood church as the liturgy of Trinity Sunday was beginning. What met our eyes stunned our expectations. In the sanctuary all seemed familiar enough: a vested presider, a quarter-century-old "temporary" altar table, an aging sister leading the song flanked by younger musicians, a man prepared to read momentarily. But the assembly! No pews, but rather a dozen school-lunchroom or bingo-hall tables and chairs, and an extraordinary group gathered restlessly around them. Most of the group were men, few over forty years of age. Women and children were nowhere to be seen. On a second survey I identified a scattering of elderly women dispersed through the crowd. Unfamiliar with the protocol of the tables, the four of us stood in the rear, aware that we had come upon something uncommon. Slowly I came to realize that the men with whom we were worshiping were mostly broken in body and spirit, some early in life by retardation and physical disabilities, others by alcohol.

The liturgy progressed as it does. The homily proclaimed the mystery of the Trinity as a mystery of divine love so limitless that it has poured out even to the poor of Bologna. Then it was time for the offering. The ushers went forward, grouping to organize themselves, and we reached for our bundles of lire. Then the unexpected happened again. The ushers also had reached for stacks of bills, and they moved through the assembly making the church's offering to the poor even as the gifts of bread and wine were being placed on the altar table. Later, on the street, we learned from another worshiper that the gift to the poor was given weekly and it was always small: a token of God's graciousness and of eschatological fullness, something to celebrate the Lord's Day in anticipation.

Where was the mystery of the Church raised up as sign of salvation to the nations ever more splendidly manifest than in this shabby group in Bologna celebrating redemptive love incarnate? Yes, corporate public ritual is always about more than immediately meets the eye.

The late Victor Turner's field work as a cultural anthropologist in West Africa resulted in his introduction into the field of ritual studies of some necessary precision in the analysis of the ritual event. Turner teaches us the value of learning to identify the smallest units within a complex ritual, the bricks or building blocks from which the whole is constructed. The Christian liturgical assembly as a ritual symbol is indeed a complex reality. Within the assembly particular roles are differentiated. Those differentiations are expressed in a variety of ways, one of the most obvious being spatial. Within the ritual space certain areas are reserved for participants with particular roles: the assembly in the nave, the presider at his chair, the musicians in the choir, the reader at the ambo. Specific people are authorized agents for specific transactions at particular moments in designated places as the liturgical action of the whole assembly unfolds.

While few participants attend in any conscious way to the precise demands on and limits to their ritual participation, departures from these demands and limits will often cause enough dissonance to make everyone involved aware of some ritual violation. Recall the bafflement within liturgical assemblies with the first appearance of lay readers. The place for reading was clearly within the designated sanctuary, but the designated sanctuary had previously been reserved for the ordained. The movement of lay readers to sanctuary space was symbolic activity of a ritual kind pointing to the kind of meaning we call theological: The distance between baptism and ordination is less than we had previously thought. When the recruitment of lay readers yielded women as well as men, the bafflement was compounded.

The question whether women should read outside the ritually designated sanctuary space demanded further probing of transcendent meaning. Yet in these simple spatial decisions the meaning of Christian baptism was being revalued, the role of the laity in the proclamation of the gospel of salvation was being recognized, the traditional ambivalence about the status of Christian women was being exposed. After two thousand years of Sunday assemblies we continue to struggle to "get it right."

Each of these ritual moments, such as the proclamation of the Scripture, involves the clustering of a set of discrete ritual symbols: ritual space like the ambo within the sanctuary; ritual roles like reader of the Holy Scripture; appropriate role performers like an ordained or baptized Christian, man or woman; ritual objects like the liturgical book containing the text to be proclaimed. But of course the trained eye learns to see more. On some occasions, but not all, this ritual moment involves additional ritual activity—processions of ministers with lighted candles, elevations of the ritual book, incensations and chants—all signifying something further about the solemnity of the occasion.

2. *Dominant Ritual Symbols:* Turner also distinguishes central ritual symbols from secondary or instrumental ones. What characterized the central symbols of a religious tradition was their further function as a kind of permanent depository for the central religious meaning of the worshiping people. Their dominance was itself signaled by the very recurrence of these ritual symbols, in higher or lower relief, in virtually every ritual event.

With that theory available to guide reflection, it has become apparent to liturgiologists that the Christian liturgy, the Church's corporate public ritual, works again and again with a central store of ritual symbols. Whatever the particular moment that calls for liturgical celebration, the Christian people know that its ritual will bring together in some distinctive combination several or all of the following elements: the assembling of believers, the waters of baptism, the oils for anointings, the bread and wine of the Eucharist, the act of laying on hands, the ritual presidency of an officeholder complemented by the ministries of the baptized, the sign of the cross, the paschal candle, the proclamation of the scriptural Word of God, and communal prayers of thanksgiving, intercession, and invocation.

During the days of the paschal Triduum, the center and the axis of all Christian liturgy, each of these dominant ritual symbols takes its turn as the center of lavish ritual elaboration: a chrism Mass for the episcopal blessing and distribution of oils; on Thursday the solemn celebration of the Eucharistic mystery itself; on Friday the solemn public veneration of the cross; on Saturday the paschal encomium in praise of the Easter light, an extravagant Liturgy of the Word with eight or twelve readings washing over the assembly in a flood of remembrance.

But there is no liturgical celebration within the whole complex of Christian sacramental rites that does not draw upon the meanings stored within these dominant ritual symbols. Crosses, for example, abound in every liturgy. The cross is carried in procession, marked large on one's own body, traced small on forehead, lips, and heart, traced over individuals and over the whole assembly. The cruciform is everywhere, from the opening rites of Christian initiation to the liturgy of Christian burial.

The secondary ritual symbols regularly serve to enhance the centrality and significance of the dominant ritual symbols. We incense the assembly and its ministers, the Book of Gospels, the bread and wine for the Eucharist and the altar table which bears them; we incense the paschal candle and the processional cross. Each of these incensations has risen from a specific moment of the Church's meeting and embracing the good in pre-Christian cultures. We have the ancient imperial courts to thank for incense; we have the peoples of

Northern Europe to praise for great liturgical fires and the Romans for bridal veilings.

3. *Rethinking Word and Sacrament:* In our recent reflection on liturgical action as patterned symbolic behavior, we have also come to examine again the classic understanding of the relationship between word and sacrament. Augustine in his treatise on the Gospel of John penned a line that would become the basis for later Scholastic sacramental theology: *Accedit verbum ad elementum, et fit Sacramentum, etiam ipsum tanquam visibile verbum.* When the word of faith is joined with the Church's gesture, the sacrament happens—a "visible word," as it were. The word of faith spoken was understood to stabilize the meaning of the ritual actions and transactions, to reduce if not eliminate confusion or ambiguity about what the Church intended in its corporate public ritual.

Several hundred years elapsed. Given the later Scholastic theologians' concern for clarity and precision, the *verbum,* or "word of faith," became equated narrowly with the "form" of the sacrament just as the *elementum,* now understood as sacral object, became the "matter" of sacramental liturgy. In this concern for precision the polyvalent nature of symbolic action was soon forgotten.

Meaning is mediated not only in the words that are said but in the tone of the speaking, in the identity of the speaker, and in the speaker's gesture, posture, and bearing in relationship to the hearers. The meaning of the formulaic "word of faith" is further enhanced but also distorted by the many other social, cultural, religious, and political meanings already present in the syntax and the lexical items that make up the verbal formula and in the visible objects and transactions to which the symbolic ritual speech refers.

Reflecting on a single incident may help to illustrate the complexity of stabilizing meaning in the actual performance of corporate public ritual. In 1988 the Episcopal Church of the Diocese of Massachusetts consecrated Barbara Harris a suffragan bishop. The liturgical assembly followed the official Episcopal rite for the ordination of a bishop. But consider how the visible presence of a black woman as the candidate for ordination reinterpreted for the assembly the meaning of the opening collect, proclaimed by the presiding bishop:

O God of unchangeable power and eternal light: Look favorably on your whole Church, that wonderful and sacred mystery; by the effectual working of your providence, carry out in tranquillity the plan of salvation; let the whole world see and know that things which we cast down are being raised up, and things which had grown old are being made new, and that all things are being brought to their perfection by him through whom all things were made, your Son Jesus Christ our Lord; who lives and reigns with you, in the unity of the Holy Spirit, one God, for ever and ever. Amen.

The prayer was no longer routinized formulaic speaking but a revelatory word.

A renewed appreciation of sacramental liturgy as the effective action of the Church alerts us to the truth that the meaning of what we do in our corporate public ritual cannot be restricted to what is said formally in ritual *praenotanda,* magisterial statement, theological tract, or official prayer text. Such discursive statements may indicate what are intended as official or normative meanings. But the available and operative meanings within an actual liturgical celebration may be both more than and also less than what is intended by officeholders who have prepared and promulgated normative liturgical books with official texts and directives for ritual performance.

4. *Saving Relationships:* The final point to be made here about the patterned activity of the liturgical assembly is that rituals are about relationships. Christian liturgical assemblies intend to set out and to celebrate relationships that save. The mystery of salvation is paschal, we say. The paschal mystery is embodied, we say, in the story of Jesus, now risen and glorified, seated at the right hand of majesty and interceding for our humankind. The paschal mystery is symbolized, we say, in the grain of wheat that falls into the ground and dies in order to bring forth life. The paschal mystery is further symbolized, we say, in this Church which is the people of God becoming the body of Christ, dying in order to rise transformed, already joined with its head in interceding for the world's salvation, continuously sent back into the world to be ambassadors of reconciliation speaking on God's behalf. But liturgy does not say these things discursively. Rather, it invites the assembly to participate together in self-engaging activity through which its members enter into and commit themselves to the

meanings and relationships that give them identity and give their lives purpose. "Who do you believe that you are and for what purpose do you live?" the contemporary inquirer might ask the Christian. The Church's corporate public worship, its symbolic ritual action, its liturgical celebrations, seeks to set out the mystery of salvation in its richness and complexity. The mystery was manifest in a Bologna parish on Trinity Sunday 1989.

Because liturgy is corporate public ritual that engages us directly, it is difficult for us to forget that the mystery is about us. We who have put on Christ nevertheless never lose the original gift of our humanity. "Every Sunday [we] dancing bears have dressed ourselves in buttoned clothes," writes Annie Dillard. "We mince around the ring on two feet. . . . Week after week Christ washes the disciples' dirty feet, handles their very toes, and repeats, 'It is all right—believe it or not—to be people.' "

*Good for the group.* We call the liturgy self-involving activity. Perhaps we can best grasp the point at issue by considering other social gatherings in which we found ourselves physically present but personally disengaged. Internally we determined to dissociate ourselves from what was happening around us, to make no commitment to it, no investment in it. We knew the danger: Once we let our guard down, once we showed the slightest interest in what was transpiring, we were hooked. Somebody smiled; we had the choice to smile back, to return a blank stare, to pretend our attention was elsewhere. A smile returned would be self-involving. Once we were hooked, we would only be drawn in further.

Liturgy is self-involving activity. The very act of assembling implies engagement with and commitment to the meanings that are going to be expressed in the assembly. The assembly itself has ritual responsibilities—the full range of things to do which we have come to call "active participation." On Sundays we crowd ourselves into rows with people we hardly know and whose company we might not normally choose. We join our voices with this company in songs of trust and praise and lament and in so doing adopt sentiments we were not previously feeling, before we assembled. We listen to sacred texts expecting to hear in them words for our lives, words that will reassure us and confirm our direction or words that will surprise us, even frighten us, with their demands on us.

We walk in processions, shout acclamations, whether halfheartedly or wholeheartedly. We take and eat the bread of the Eucharist and proclaim it the Body of Christ broken for us. We drink from the cup of the new covenant and so bind ourselves to the law of Christ. We remember Jesus Christ by voicing our gratitude to the God he called "Abba," uncommon father. We ask that God's will for the world's healing be done in us and through us. And we let ourselves be sent from the assembly for just that purpose.

Why do we do these things? Hazel Motes, a character in Flannery O'Connor's short novel *Wise Blood,* engaged in some bizarre rituals that caused his landlady to protest, "There's no reason for it. People have quit doing it." To which he replied wisely, "They ain't quit doing it as long as I'm doing it." In fact, the landlady was partially right. Wearing barbed wire next to one's flesh is not socially acceptable penitential behavior. But people everywhere are assembling on Sundays to engage in other kinds of ritual behavior for what they believe is some good purpose.

I identify that purpose in two phrases: Such liturgical activity *confirms group identity* and *advances group goals*. The corporate public rites help us to remember together who we are. And in the remembering through ritual doing we reinvest ourselves in a pattern for our lives. Week by week, year by year, little by little but more and more, we put on the mind of Christ and become his body because we trust this is the way of salvation.

### Summary and Conclusion

We will reflect further on this dual outcome of our corporate public worship in the next chapter. For the present we can sum up something of what we have learned in the past twenty-five years since the promulgation of *Sacrosanctum Concilium.* We have learned much that is helpful by expanding our understanding of the field of liturgical study. We have come to recognize that our sacred sacramental activity is sacred and sacramental precisely as corporate public ritual of the kind all human peoples engage in. "It is all right—believe it or not—to be people."

Twenty-five years into liturgical renewal we see that our liturgy may be helpfully understood as "an assembly of people who gather when it is timely in order to engage in patterned behavior which is valued because it is good for the group since it promotes group identity and advances group goals." Next we will take up the question of how the corporate public ritual of the Church, its sacramental liturgy, "promotes group identity and advances group goals." The language is ordinary. The topic itself is fully theological.

## Suggestions for Further Reading

Dillard, Annie. "An Expedition to the Pole," *Teaching a Stone to Talk*. New York: Harper & Row, 1982. A meditation on the mystery of public worship by a Pulitzer prize winning author who has a contemplative eye and a keen pen.

*Liturgy: The Holy Cross*. Washington: The Liturgical Conference, 1980.

*Liturgy: Central Symbols*. Washington: The Liturgical Conference, 1987. Each volume in this series provides extensive historical, theological, biblical, and catechetical background for an in-depth understanding of liturgical symbols.

# 4

## Eucharistic Praying
## and the Good of the Church

It may go without saying that our Eucharistic praying is for the good of the Church. Did we ever doubt it, before, during, or after the Council? Was that not the very premise of the reform of the Mass? Because the bishops knew in faith that the Mass was good for the Church, they mandated fuller participation for the laity in the Mass. They even mandated a structural reform which made the laity's participation integral to the basic unfolding of the rite. Because the good of Eucharistic worship seems self-evident, the discussion of the topic in this series on what we have learned about Roman Catholic liturgy since Vatican II may appear pointless.

Yet however pointless it might seem to raise the question about the good of the Eucharist, I want to question what we have come to consider self-evident. In what way is it the case that Eucharistic praying is good for the Church? I propose to explore the good of the Eucharist in the context of the previous discussion of corporate public ritual. The Roman Catholic Eucharistic liturgy, as corporate public ritual, involves "an assembly of people who, when it is timely, engage in patterned behavior valued as good for the group because it confirms group identity and advances group goals." What needs to be explored here is the meaning involved in the affirmation that our Eucharist both "confirms group identity" and "advances group goals."

## The Centrality of the Sunday Eucharist

University of Chicago anthropologist Clifford Geertz in an extended essay on religion as a cultural system affirms two things related to our question. First, he argues that the central meanings and beliefs of a people's faith are most effectively communicated through rituals. This is so, we might note, because ritual is self-engaging activity that causes people to invest themselves personally in what the rituals express. Secondly, he notes that among a believing people's liturgical rites, one will stand out as the center of the whole repertoire of rites for which the people assemble.

Now, in *Sacrosanctum Concilium* we find Geertz's anthropological theory confirmed in several ways. The first chapter affirms the centrality of the liturgy among the various activities in which the Church engages. The bishops in council called liturgy "the summit toward which the activity of the Church is directed" and also "the fountain from which all her power flows" (*SC* 10). This is language many theologians have subsequently judged extravagant, even though cultural anthropologists would heartily concur with it. But the Constitution on the Sacred Liturgy becomes even more specific. It is not any and every liturgical rite or even any and every Eucharistic celebration that is central. Rather, the constitution focuses on the Sunday Eucharist. The Council teaches that "by an apostolic tradition which took its origin from the very day of Christ's resurrection, the Church celebrates the paschal mystery every eighth day" (*SC* 106). And then they continue:

> . . . on this day Christ's faithful should come together into one place so that, by hearing the word of God and taking part in the Eucharist, they may call to mind the passion, the resurrection, and the glorification of the Lord Jesus, and may thank God who "has begotten us again, through the resurrection of Jesus Christ, from the dead, unto a living hope" (I Pet 1:3).

Geertz's second point is thereby affirmed. Among all the many liturgical rites we celebrate as good for the Church, one stands out: the Sunday Eucharist. Our working definition is also corroborated. Corporate public ritual requires an assembly "when it is timely." The Catholic people have long known a distinction between frequent, even daily, celebration of the Eucharist, which is devotional, and the Sunday Eucharistic assembly, which is vital. We have even been prepared to say that the consequences of unnecessary absence from that assembly are deadly, mortal. In the language of the constitution, "This day [Sunday] the original feast day . . . is the foundation and nucleus of the whole liturgical year" (106).

The commission that was asked to undertake the reform of the Missal understood the point clearly. Fr. Frederick McManus, an American liturgical *peritus,* or expert, has narrated how the group determined early that Eucharistic reform, the "new order of the Mass," would assume as the normative Eucharistic liturgy the Sunday Mass in the local parish. This is the heart of the Catholic repertoire of corporate public rituals. This focusing of the reform serves to indicate when and how the Catholic people as a people are most fully engaged in praying Eucharistically. Catholics gather for Sunday Eucharist in their parish churches. They do so innocent of the demands of anthropological ritual theory. They do so because it is good for them. Our concern now is to reflect further on why this is the case. What is the good that is valued, sought, and realized?

### The Path to the Eucharistic Center

We will proceed to consider the Sunday Eucharistic center of Catholic life by following the path to the center. A worship system that has a center has structural elements that support that center. So the Church assembles when it is timely to make Eucharist. But it also gathers on other occasions for other liturgical events, and these are always directed toward the Sunday Eucharistic assembly. Our familiar speech gives us away. We talk about the Mass and the sacraments, setting the Eucharist apart. Our explanations for that distinction are generally theological. We talk about a Eucharistic real presence of the risen Christ Jesus which we have wished to distinguish from Christ's saving presence in the other sacramental activity of the Church. Here we will make the distinction not on the basis of theological claims but solely on the basis of cultural and ritual theory. This theory does not negate the distinction reflected in our theological speaking about the Mass and the sacraments but serves instead to confirm it.

Since 1972 we have had a new order for Christian initiation that sets out a process for bringing new believers first to the Sunday assembly and its Liturgy of the Word and eventually to the fullness of its Eucharistic action. This initiatory process is punctuated by a series of liturgical rites which anticipate some but not all of the ritual patterns and ritual transactions of the Sunday Eucharist. Signing the candidates with the cross, the ritual proclamation of the Word of God, and prayers of intercession are the central acts of the liturgical assembly for the enrollment of the catechumens. Subsequently, the catechumens are assembled again and again, and in these subsequent assemblies the Church celebrates the Word with them, lays hands on them in prayer for their spiritual healing and blessing, anoints them for their strengthening, and eventually invites them to recite the Lord's Prayer and the Creed in the assembly.

The catechumens are always invited to the Sunday assembly for the Liturgy of the Word, but the assembly dismisses them at midpoint just as it starts its Eucharistic liturgy. All of this non-Eucharistic liturgical gathering is leading ineluctably through the waters of baptism and the sealing of confirmation to full participation in the Sunday Eucharist. The rites of Christian initiation do not stand apart ritually as ends in themselves; they are part of a liturgical system which has a center.

The Church also assembles ritually to attend to the separation of some of its members from the Sunday assembly, whether because of sin, illness, or death. When sin separates and divides the Church, it celebrates liturgical rites of reconciliation. Although there is great controversy about the adequacy of the 1969 reformed order for recon ciliation, it can be fairly said that the Church is newly aware since the liturgical reform of the sacrament of penance that reconciliation is an act of the Church effected through the prayer of the Church assembled. It is that very awareness that has given rise to calls for new forms of reconciliation for those alienated from the Church. These assemblies for reconciliation are directed to the reconstituting of the Eucharistic assembly in its fullness. Rites of reconciliation do not stand apart ritually as ends in themselves. They are part of a liturgical system that has a Eucharistic center.

Moreover, since the liturgical reforms of Vatican II we have recovered a better awareness of the liturgical nature of the Church's pastoral ministry to the sick and the elderly who cannot attend the Sunday assembly. We name the absent sick and elderly in our praying of general intercessions, and we send parish ministers to join them in their homes in the name of the Church as an extension of the Sunday assembly. The 1974 order for the pastoral care and anointing of the sick understands that small domestic gatherings with the sick for the reading of Scripture, for prayer, and for Communion are part of its official liturgy, even when the ministers are lay members of the Sunday Eucharistic community and not the pastor. The reformed liturgical order for the anointing of the sick specifies that family members, caregivers, even neighbors, are to assemble with the priest to pray in the name of the Church so that those who are sick might be restored to their rightful places in the Sunday Eucharistic assembly.

And when Christians die, the reformed rites provide for the assembling of believers to pray, and by that praying to commend the dying publicly to God's mercy. Viaticum is offered as food for the journey into the heavenly kingdom. But funeral rites, too, lead toward Eucharist. In the rites of Christian burial, the next-to-final gathering with the body takes place where the Sunday Eucharistic assembly occurs, an acknowledgement of the sacramental center of a Christian life now brought to its end but also brought to the unending heavenly banquet long anticipated in each Eucharist.

Furthermore, Catholics gather at the Eucharist to celebrate the most secular of sacraments, the sacrament of a Christian marriage. The mystery of marriage is fully paschal: Two persons give their own lives for the life of the world. The Church gathers to pray on their behalf and to witness their act of faith that God continues to effect the world's salvation through love—but the kind of "harsh and dreadful love" which the late Dorothy Day contrasted with storybook romance. The love of disciples in a Christian marriage sets out for the world the mystery that new life comes through readiness to wager one's own dying. Marriage is the secular sacrament of the paschal mystery. The Eucharistic setting in which Christian marriage is ritually enacted interprets the redemptive significance of risky love. The weekly Sunday Eucharist of married Christians helps them remember and even intensifies their understanding of the mystery that gives meaning to their lives.

The Church also assembles when it is timely for rites of ordination. These liturgical acts, too, are not ends in themselves. The Catholic tradition early on rejected "absolute ordination" and has consistently corrected itself when it lapsed into treating ordination as end and not means. When the Church assembles to ordain deacons, presbyters, and bishops, it does so because of the need of the Christian people to be well served, to be well guided in their lives, and to be well gathered for Sunday Eucharistic worship.

## Eucharistic Liturgy: The Church Constituting Itself

What is going on here? According to the explanation of the cultural theorists, two characteristic features of ritual systems can be noted here. These give us insight into the way we worship as a Church. It is inevitable that liturgy will be both repetitive and redundant. At first hearing these may seem to be negative judgments. But the theorists consider repetition and redundancy benign features of corporate public ritual.

Redundancy means simply that a single truth—a single mystery— is being set out in a variety of ways. There may be many forms of ritual symbolic expression, but there is only one reality being signified. Liturgies of initiation, liturgies of reconciliation, liturgies for the sick, all mean to engage the Church assembled in the mystery of Christ—now under one aspect, then another. Yet there is no other ultimate meaning than the mystery of salvation. This is what every liturgical rite means to mediate.

Repetition means that the Church engages itself again and again, week by week, year by year, in a limited range of rites it has agreed upon as effective mediators of what it believes in, hopes for, and loves. Whenever the Church initiates new members, it repeats the same pattern of rites; whenever it reconciles, it performs the same core ritual actions, pronounces the same ritual words, uses the same gestures. When its rituals point to the immediate meaning of ecclesial reconciliation, they point also to the ultimate meaning of salvation in Christ.

Repetition also means that the Church expresses its meanings again and again through a limited number of core ritual symbols. Consider the sign of the cross traced on our bodies, on our foreheads, the cross held up before us in procession, the cross venerated, the cruciform shaping the very space within which Christians gather for worship. Or the Scriptures again and again held high for veneration, incensed and surrounded by lights, unfailingly proclaimed and received in the liturgical assembly as the Word of God. Or the Church assembling again and again on every Lord's Day because it is timely to do so.

Repetition and redundancy are benign characteristics of liturgical activity because they serve the purpose of anamnesis. Anamnesis is biblical language which was long ago taken up by the Church and recently recovered as liturgical language. But it is also philosophical and liturgical language of a technical sort, which refers to a distinctive feature of human behavior. We can perhaps best understand anamnesis by considering it indirectly. Anamnesis speaks about a distinctive kind of human remembering. In common speech we are more likely to talk about its opposite, amnesia.

We are familiar with the disorder of clinical amnesia, a diagnosis given to name a memory lapse of a crucial kind. The amnesiac is not the person who has misplaced her glasses one time too many. She is the person who has forgotten who she is. She has lost her conscious awareness of the basic relationships that give her her identity. The amnesiac cannot answer when asked who are you? where have you come from? where are you headed? who are your parents? have you any family? where is your home? what kind of work do you do?

"Anamnesis" and "amnesia" come from a common Greek root. The biblical and liturgical use of the word "anamnesis" rises from a perception that there is a disorder analogous to clinical amnesia that plagues the human community. To be human is to be threatened with spiritual amnesia. At the level of our spiritual identity we do not remember for long who we really are. Those ultimate relationships that give us our spiritual identity slip from consciousness all too easily, and we lapse into noncomprehension about our deepest identity.

Corporate public ritual brings us together to participate actively in the relationships that identify us spiritually. Liturgical rites provide self-engaging activity of a symbolic form which points us to and engages us personally in the mystery within which we live. For it is both our faith and our experience that the mystery of Christ is always present. But it is equally our experience that we are inattentive to the truth of our origins and our destiny. We forget who we are, where we came from, where we are headed. So we assemble when it is timely to invest ourselves as a community of Christians in liturgical anamnesis. The self-engaging activity of our liturgy not only causes us to remember who we are; it invites us to commit ourselves to a life congruent with our identity.

All liturgy is anamnesis. Sunday Eucharist is the center of Christian anamnesis. This is the weekly occasion on which the baptized assemble together to reconstitute themselves publicly in their identity as the Church of Jesus Christ. The Church is reconstituting itself publicly, attempting to put on the mind of Christ ritually, when it celebrates the Liturgy of the Word. The Church is reconstituting itself as a priestly people when it prays the prayer of general intercession. As a priestly people, it intercedes with God in Christ's name—"hear our prayer . . . hear our prayer . . . hear our prayer"—for the world's healing and salvation.

But the Church acts most profoundly in the Sunday assembly to reconstitute itself as the body of Christ. In Sunday Eucharistic liturgy we move through public praise and thanksgiving for the mystery; we remember, and remembering dare to move even nearer to our shared identification in the mystery of Christ. Through sacramental Communion in the Body broken for the world's life and the Blood poured out for the world's forgiveness, each of us engages ourselves, each of us commits ourselves, and the Church is reconstituted by God's gift to us.

Our constitution as Church is always partial, never exhaustive. So we must reassemble every Lord's Day. We are burdened by the limits of our comprehension of inexhaustible mystery. We are also limited by the inauthenticity which comes from having divided identities, dual commitments to serve our own purposes as well as God's.

Annie Dillard's compassionate vision and gift of language helps us to see ourselves as we might be seen by the God who assembles us week by week to make Eucharist.

> Why do we people in churches seem like cheerful, brainless tourists on a packaged tour of the Absolute? . . .
>
> On the whole, I do not find Christians, outside of the catacombs, sufficiently sensible of conditions. Does anyone have the foggiest idea what sort of power we so blithely invoke? Or, as I suspect, does no one believe a word of it? The churches are children playing on the floor with their chemistry sets, mixing up a batch of TNT to kill a Sunday morning. It is madness to wear ladies' straw hats and velvet hats to church; we should all be wearing crash helmets. Ushers should issue life preservers and signal flares; they should lash us to our pews" (*Teaching a Stone to Talk*).

We who are the Church of Jesus Christ scarcely recognize our own halfhearted complacency when we approach the altar of sacrifice Sunday by Sunday to commune in the Body and Blood of the Lamb who was slain.

The initial impetus of the liturgical reform which produced the new *ordo Missae* acknowledged the need for strong symbolic forms which would be capable of engaging us, capable of penetrating our spiritual amnesia. The people who are the Church are themselves to bring the gifts to the altar; their gifts should include money offered for the poor (see GIRM 49). The people assembled are to sing acclamations throughout the Eucharistic prayer, involving themselves thereby in the praise of God who has called them to be Church (see GIRM 55). The bread of the Eucharist should look like bread and taste like bread; the fragments to be eaten by the ecclesial body of Christ should be broken from the one loaf so that we get the point of our oneness with Christ (see GIRM 56). The laity should—after many centuries of exclusion from an evangelically mandated ritual action, "Take, all of you, and drink"—each drink, one by one, from the cup of the covenant (see GIRM 240). Such drinking might stimulate our dulled minds and provoke us to wonder: To what are we committing ourselves when we commune in the Blood of Christ?

**Praxis and Theory**

So much for the theory. What of the praxis? Having explored from the viewpoint of ritual theory the fundamental soundness of the liturgical reform of Vatican II, we can now wonder together why dioceses, parishes, and national Churches are reporting that they are at a kind of liturgical impasse. Nothing seems to be happening, so the common lament goes. If the theory is sound, the question rises, why is our ecclesial and liturgical renewal stalemated?

I turn to further theory to propose some ideas for consideration. My persistent use of anthropological and ritual theory is not meant to displace our theological understandings of divine mystery. In my judgment the theory affirms our basic theological claim that grace does not overwhelm our humanity but surrounds us and invites us. Response to grace involves us in acts of self-transcendence, movement beyond ourselves. But as a Church, it seems that it is just that movement beyond ourselves that we are refusing.

As a Church, clergy and lay, we persist in our operative disbelief that the body mediates spiritual experience and insight. We profess faith in the goodness of creation; we laud the anti-Docetist attitudes of the early Church Fathers against the Gnostics; we hand on from generation to generation the claim that the sacraments are outward signs that give grace. But really, we seem to believe almost none of it. We are Docetists to the core. Liturgy is about bodily prayer, and we continue to minimize bodiliness, only "seeming" to engage flesh and bone, blood and sinew.

Having proclaimed in the General Instruction on the Roman Missal the importance of a strong bread sign, bread of quality that can be broken and eaten, we immediately gave ourselves permission as a Church to persist in our Docetism. The compromise written into GIRM 283 that small hosts may yet be used "for pastoral reasons" has been read everywhere as authorization to evade the norm. Local Churches that have tried to celebrate the Sunday Eucharist with bread of quality have been subjected to official suspicion and scrutiny, as though they were deviants. Only a few presiders have ever taken care to provide a full loaf and then taken time for the careful ritual breaking of the bread prior to the invitation to Eucharistic Communion. Even fewer have persisted for fifteen years and more in the enactment of this rite in the Sunday assembly. Those who have persisted are considered affected, even precious, in their liturgical behavior.

Docetist liturgists is what we are as a Church, despite the fact that "Docetist liturgist" is an oxymoron. In many Churches the Eucharistic cup has not yet been restored to the members of the Sunday Eucharistic assembly. We justify this flagrant liturgical abuse with doctrinal arguments: the doctrine of concomitance means that it is enough to provide only a single element in order to receive the whole Christ. The doctrine may be impeccable; the sacramental theory is unsound.

To bolster the right to liturgical deviance regarding Eucharistic cupsharing, claims of pastoral necessity are introduced. "The parish cannot afford to be paying for altar wine for everyone." "The people cannot be asked to stay the extra time the use of the cup would require." "We do not have enough priests around, and our people do not like receiving Communion from anybody but the priest." "The people have not expressed any need for the cup, so there is no point in introducing it just for the sake of novelty." "The people are afraid of contagious disease, and there is no reason to upset them at Communion with health scares.''

All the excuses are only that. At the bottom, we do not really have faith in the sacramental principle. We do not believe that earthly realities like the peace passed among strangers, a loaf broken and shared, and the cup passed among us in memory of Jesus really tell us anything about ourselves and our place in the mystery of salvation. We really think that anything worth knowing about salvation is to be found in books or heard in lectures and sermons. We do not trust God to speak to us through our bodies. We do not yet believe that saving grace is mediated to us and through us for the world's salvation in anything so accessible as corporate public ritual. So we promote a reform and resist it, and we wonder why it bears so little fruit. We ought not to be so surprised.

Deny the Church assembled on Sunday the fullness of the bread sign in its celebration of the mystery of Christ. Deny the fullness of the bread sign and offer instead as an alternate sign of Communion in the mystery of salvation tasteless individual wafers that have been reserved in the tabernacle. But do not then wonder why the liturgical reform makes us neither robust Christians nor united as a Church. Deny the Church assembled on Sunday its regular share in the Blood of Christ. Deny the cup of the new covenant, but then do not wonder why the laity seem halfhearted in their commitment to discipleship. Enough has been said to illustrate my point. Our theory and our praxis are disconnected. But the theory proves itself even in its being ignored in our pastoral praxis.

### Summary and Conclusions: What Have We Learned?

However partial our comprehension of what it means to be the ecclesial body of Christ, we assemble Sunday by Sunday and on other occasions too, when it is timely, to engage in corporate public ritual. We engage in ritual anamnesis not simply because someone else judges that we have to. We explore ritually and symbolically our place in the mystery of salvation, because this liturgical work is vital to our very existence as a Church. In our assembling and acting together, our identity as the Church of Jesus Christ is confirmed. In our assembling and acting together, we are becoming the Church of Jesus Christ in this time and place.

The liturgical reform of Vatican II placed great emphasis on lay participation in the Eucharistic liturgy. From the viewpoint of ritual theory the decision was sound. The Church reconstitutes itself week by week as the Church of Jesus Christ, as a covenant people, as a community of disciples through its corporate public ritual. We are still learning to trust ourselves to the dynamic vision of the liturgical reform twenty-five years later. We are still learning to risk ourselves, as a Church, to sacramental mystery.

## Suggestions for Further Reading

The introductions *(praenotanda)* to each of the reformed Roman liturgical books are not yet widely read, even by many persons who exercise leadership in planning or in presiding at public worhsip. At least the *General Instruction on the Roman Missal* (1970), the introduction to the *Lectionary,* (2nd edition), the introduction to the *Rite for the Christian Initiation of Adults* (1988) deserve wide reading. Study editions of these documents are available from the Publications Office of the National Conference of Catholic Bishops.

Geertz, Clifford. "Religion as a Cultural System," *The Interpretation of Cultures.* New York: Basic Books, 1973.

Grimes, Ronald. "Sitting and Eating," *Beginnings in Ritual Studies.* Washington: University Press of America, 1982. Considers differing styles of ritual embodiment, noting how Catholic embodiment finds its ritual and symbolic center in eating.

Ross, Susan. " 'Then honor God in your body' (1 Cor 6:20): Feminist and Sacramental Theology on the Body," *Horizons* 16 (Spring 1989) 7–27. Explores in what ways feminist theologians would fault the classical sacramental vision of the embodiment of divine mystery.

# 5

---

# *Liturgical Language: The Words of Faith*

We assemble when it is timely to engage in patterned behavior that we value as good for the Church. One aspect of that patterned ritual behavior is our ritual speaking. Not only do we move in sacred space and handle holy things but we engage in sacred speaking. In this chapter we will consider liturgical language, the words of our public worship.

The issue is complex; we will make some necessary distinctions in order to clarify the complexity. We will first distinguish between discursive and presentational language, and we will call liturgical language "presentational." We will also distinguish between metaphoric and symbolic presentations and will explain that liturgical language is symbolic. We will then distinguish between verbal and nonverbal symbolic presentations of mystery and show the relationship between them. Finally we will argue that the Church is essentially a community of language and, further, that the common language of the Church's worship is neither Latin nor English nor Spanish but its repertoire of common symbols, verbal and nonverbal. To illustrate this we will look at the one example of the emerging vocabulary of the post-Communion prayer. Throughout this discussion we will be trying to assess our current situation with the development of English as a liturgical language.

### Vatican II and the Development of Liturgical English

Our reflection must begin by noting our current situation twenty-five years after *Sacrosanctum Concilium*. The move to develop a liturgical English began officially in 1963 when the bishops who gathered in council in St. Peter's voted affirmatively on the second paragraph of article 36 of *SC*. The first paragraph stated as a controlling norm, "The use of the Latin language is to be preserved in the Latin rite." Then the second paragraph boldly stated the value of departing from the norm:

> But since the use of the mother tongue, whether in the Mass, the administration of the sacraments, or other parts of the liturgy, frequently may be of great advantage to the people, the limits of its employment may be extended. This will apply in the first place to the readings and directives, and to some of the prayers and chants, according to the regulations on this matter to be laid down separately in subsequent chapters.

The third paragraph invited the Roman Church to become polyglot: "It is for the competent territorial ecclesiastical authorities . . . to decide whether, and to what extent, the vernacular language is to be used according to these norms." Something of the story of what happened next is common knowledge: English-speaking bishops who had been talking together and watching developments since the first session of the Council in 1962 brought their episcopal conferences to establish the International Committee on English in the Liturgy. And so ICEL was born. The work began to make the English speech of our public life the language of our public prayer.

More than a few times during the past quarter century critics have challenged the wisdom of trying to develop an international English for the liturgical assembly. The skeptics have said that it cannot be done. They point out correctly that language is culturally grounded and that the cultures of Ireland and the United States, of Australia and South Africa, of the Philippines and Pakistan, of Great Britain and India, are vastly different. It is only historical exigency, say the skeptics and critics, that has resulted in its coming to pass that the official language of public life in each of these countries is English. A common public language that is the byproduct of colonialism only masks difference; it does not remove it.

Ordinary experience seems to confirm the truth of the skeptic's viewpoint. All English speakers who have traveled widely can tell tales about listening to another English speaker whose idiom and diction were virtually unintelligible. A prominent French publishing house notes when one of its authors' writings is "translated from the American." In Ireland, but hardly in the urban United States, it is possible to sing meaningfully of "Christ my lantern." But that very familiar experience of our social and cultural differences can bring us to an important realization: liturgical English has a unique purpose. The common referent of all liturgical speaking is transcendent mystery, the mystery of Christ. We presume to do no more and no less in the liturgical assembly than to speak publicly of the ineffable, to name our relationship to what is essentially nameless and unnameable.

In an earlier generation we had presumed that speaking of ineffable mystery had been taken care of through the crafting of a peculiar language called liturgical Latin. But, unexpectedly, the English of everyday speaking, the English of commerce and popular culture, the language of bureaucratic obfuscation and journalistic oversimplification, a vigorous language quite capable of naming every profane reality in all its nuances, is being impressed into divine service.

I deliberately use the military metaphor. Conscription normally involves the enlisting of the undisciplined, and a regimen of discipline follows. The conscript has to be matched to the task. Analogously, we as Church must provide for ourselves a disciplined language for public prayer. We are being challenged in this generation to find ways to use our wonderfully profane cosmopolitan language to speak of the transcendent. We believe we live within the mystery of Christ. We believe the saving mystery is being made manifest in every culture even as it transcends them all. We must bring the experience of the mystery to ritual speech in our own public tongue.

How can it be done? When Moses assembled the people at the foot of Mount Sinai, he managed—or was it Aaron?—to speak of YHWH's self-disclosure through the vocabulary of political conquest and international commerce that the ordinary Hebrew people understood. Later, the seventy Jewish scribes of the Diaspora found out how to make the Greek used in Mediterranean commerce work for the public reading of the Torah in the synagogue after the ancient Hebrew language had vanished from the people's memories. Still later,

Pope St. Leo the Great took the public language of the declining Roman Empire and reinvigorated it for use in the liturgical assembly to speak of the Eucharistic mystery. Even closer to our day but still centuries ago, Thomas Cranmer put the language of Shakespeare's England to work, as he crafted prayers for the cathedrals, the minsters, and the chapels of the English countryside. But the very mention of Moses, the seventy scribes of the Jewish Diaspora, St. Leo the Great, and Thomas Cranmer tells us that only a few generations in human history are faced with the challenge of creating a language for worship. In between times in most generations, worshipers gathered in public assembly draw on the accumulated capital of a stable tradition of public religious language.

## Discursive and Presentational Language

We happen to be living in one of those odd generations. So at least some among us must become critically conscious of how language works and how the religious language of public ritual works in order to craft it appropriately for liturgical use. A first distinction to attend to is the distinction between discursive and presentational uses of language. What is the point of the distinction? Modern linguistic analysis values language that is capable of setting out clear ideas through verbal forms whose meaning is precise and whose orderly syntax governs the relationship of ideas in such a way that misunderstanding is all but precluded. This is the language of discourse, the language of the academic lecture, of the law, of science. When suitable words are chosen and arranged in the required order, our thoughts are communicable as statements of fact or questions about what can be verified.

But the linguistic analysts acknowledge that very few of our daily verbal acts follow the rules of discourse. Even less of our liturgical language does. "Holy, holy, holy," we cry. "Heaven and earth are full of your glory." "Earth" we know. But what precisely is "heaven" or "glory" or "holiness"? Language philosophers have tried to account for all these other ways we use words. The most harsh-sounding judgment is that such verbal activity is meaningless, that is, that it operates outside the rules for communicating ideas. A more benign-sounding judgment calls our nonconforming language "expressive," expressing feelings but not ideas. But either way the judgment is that such language does not deal with cognitive content because it does not communicate information that can be verified.

But when believers in liturgical assembly cry

> *"Kadosh, kadosh, kadosh"*
> *"Hagios, hagios, hagios"*
> *"Sanctus, sanctus, sanctus"*
> "Holy, holy, holy"

they are not persuaded that their speech is meaningless. Neither are all philosophers of language. A philosopher like Suzanne Langer prefers to speak of presentational uses of language, uses which are most familiar to us through our processes of naming and our use of metaphor. More about these shortly. More immediately our focus is on what we are doing with "Holy, holy, holy."

First, we must take account of the fact that such speaking is not original with us. These phrases are part of a tradition of liturgical speaking that originated with Isaiah in the Temple as he responded to his perception of the presence of ineffable mystery (see Isa 6). Language used presentationally respects perceptions, for perceptions rise from experience. But perceptions and experiences are fleeting if we do not name them. By naming them we intend to get a handle on them. We acknowledge their presence, move out toward them to appropriate them and to respond to them.

In our everyday language use, such naming of fleeting perceptions grounded in experience has been called "prelude to cognition." Children demand the names of things. We all bring experience from silence to speech and then to thought. Such naming is always partial. Our words catch only aspects of what we perceive to be our experience. When we make a next move to bring perceptions to the clarity of thought, we leave even more of the originating experience behind. Something is gained, something is lost, in the move from perception to naming to discourse.

Yet when what is perceived is the ineffable—the living God— naming is never a prelude to knowing clearly. For by definition the ineffable cannot be comprehended by human discourse. Isaiah cannot name the living God; he can only utter language that acknowledges unnameable divine presence. Such first-order religious language is the kind of language we normally use in worship. In our worship tradition we imitate Isaiah's act of worship with comparable utterances. Our liturgical language is essentially presentational. It is not discourse about God, not clear communication of verifiable information about God. But it is not meaningless. Our liturgical talking is presentational; it rises from religious experience.

Rosemary Haughton once described our public religious language as language borrowed from those who have been transformed by their experience of God. When such words as Isaiah's become part of the tradition of speech for public worship, they are given to the rest of us as formative speech which helps us name our own fleeting perceptions of mystery and which anticipates for us our own radical transformations. Religious speech is put on our lips to resound in our ears and so to penetrate our minds and hearts.

## Metaphors and Symbols

Much of the presentational language that gains a place in the tradition of public worship takes the form of metaphor. Metaphor goes beyond naming. Naming is a use of words that merely point to our perceptions of reality. Metaphor happens through a more-complex speech event in which insight comes precisely because of the tension produced by talking about two different things at the same time, for example, "conscripting the English language for divine service."

Consider the emergence of the dominant biblical metaphor "covenant" in the thirteenth century B.C. The place was the desert of the Sinai peninsula; the time, the weeks and months after the Hebrew people went out from bondage under Pharoah. "What is going on here?" the Hebrew people asked Moses. Moses must have asked himself the same thing many times as he struggled with Pharoah, led a quarrelsome and not very grateful people to freedom, and then camped with them at the foot of Mount Sinai.

Then one day Moses went up the mountain, to a place of meeting. Self-identified as an ungifted speaker who preferred to let Aaron do the talking, Moses (or was it Aaron?) was nevertheless moved to metaphor. "God is giving us a covenant," he said, in a clearly inspired speech act which gave himself and then the people insight into what was going on. The normal field of meaning for "convenant" lay in the worlds of political conquest, commercial transaction, and domestic relations. Moses associated the people's experience of God with their many experiences of human covenant negotiation. The metaphor caught their attention, so that the people could acknowledge and respond to the ineffable mystery that was disrupting their lives. The new situation was slowly becoming more intelligible. No longer in bondage to Pharoah, the Hebrew people were being invited to bind themselves to the One whose power to save they had already experienced. It was becoming clearer what kind of relationship they were involved in.

Gail Ramshaw writes, "A religious tradition is an historical adherence to a set of metaphors: wholly to alter the metaphors would be to change the religion." Certainly the covenant metaphor is central to all biblical religions and functions as a central ritual concept. But I think that literary critic Philip Wheelwright introduces a further helpful precision by distinguishing metaphor and symbol. Good metaphors may capture a unique flash of insight that serves no lasting public purpose. By contrast, the symbols of a people express relatively stable insights.

Religious symbols—I would call "covenant" such a symbol—present some recurrent, transgenerational element of a people's experience of the living God. Covenant is the public symbol of an abiding relationship originally perceived by Moses in the unfolding of events from the revelation at the burning bush to the journey to Sinai, a relationship whose terms were reinterpreted by Jesus, a relationship which still has the power to bind and to free believers today. Ritual language, the language of the liturgy, must have the stability characteristic of symbol. It must be stable in its referent and stabilizing in its use. It must have the power to guide people to recognize their own experiences of the living God as they bring their perceptions from silence to public speaking. In this last quarter of the twentieth century Christian people are learning anew the shared symbols of a common faith.

## Verbal and Nonverbal Symbols in the Liturgy

The requirement of the verbal symbols of a religion (like "covenant" or "Lamb of God") that they be stable in their referents itself requires some explanation. Symbolic speech, stabilized in the language of public prayer, is essentially metaphoric in its impulses. Prayer language, with its clear and distinct ideas, is an alternative to precise discourse. But it is the only kind of speaking possible when the referent is always inexhaustible and incomprehensible mystery, yet mystery present and available to people in their lives. Metaphor unites unlikes, and in the fusion reaction that metaphor unleashes, insight is produced. "This bread is the Body of Christ," we say.

Metaphor pairs unlikes, and each of the unlikes in the pair has its own independent field of meaning before it is forced into this match. Every metaphor is polysemous, full of meaning; it has a surplus of meaning beyond what its original speaker sought in the match. The metaphor become public symbol becomes a constant in the repertoire of religious speech, but the potential for further insight perdures. "We who eat this bread become the body of Christ," we say. "Because we are all one body," we say, "we must eat from this one bread."

In the liturgical assembly we pair verbal and nonverbal symbols, and as we attend them, we let them interpret each other. We count on the tradition of insight to express and strengthen our faith, and we are happily surprised when from time to time our ritual pairing of symbolic forms discloses unexpected meanings. Most of these are fleeting, but occasionally the tradition of meanings itself is permanently expanded.

A fleeting insight: On Good Friday a severely disabled adult spotted the massive wooden cross, something new in a sanctuary otherwise familiar to him. He stood at a ritually inappropriate moment, interrupting the flow of the official liturgy, and imitated its cruciform with his own flailing limbs. Did he retain insight beyond the moment? The liturgical rite itself was not modified. Yet I recall his gift of insight every year when the stark cruciform commands our attention on Good Friday.

The verbal symbols, tensive and expansive by definition, nevertheless work in liturgy to stabilize the public meanings that constitute our common faith. "Behold the wood of the cross on which hung the Savior of the world." We repeat the verbal refrain as we carry the cross in procession and then line ourselves up to venerate it. Were there no stable public meanings, we would cease to be a community of faith. We would not be able to proclaim our faith publicly; we would not be able to connect our own experiences of ineffable mystery to decisive events of God's self-disclosure.

The insights of successive generations accrue, and a tradition of verbal and nonverbal symbols takes shape. The meaning fields of traditional symbols expand and contract, rising and receding from ecclesial consciousness as our cultural experiences shift. Sometimes the verbal and nonverbal symbols are themselves disconnected from each other for centuries, displaced by some other insight which at the time overshadowed the originally intended one. We have never ceased to repeat the dominical invitation:

> Take this, all of you, and drink from it:
> this is the cup of my blood,
> the blood of the new and everlasting covenant.
> It will be shed for you and for all
> so that sins may be forgiven.
> Do this in memory of me.

Yet how odd our behavior in the face of the proclamation! For centuries we Roman Catholics have said the words and then done nothing, interrupting the power of both the verbal symbol of covenant and the nonverbal symbol of the shared cup. *"Accedit verbum ad elementum fit sacramentum"* was Augustine's formula for sacramental efficacy. When the verbal symbols and the nonverbal symbols are paired, the Church is effectively brought into contact with divine mystery. While we have taught Augustine's axiom faithfully, our liturgical praxis suggests that we continue to miss his meaning.

## The Common Language of Catholic Worship

So far we have sketched, however briefly, the realization that the common language of the Catholic people at worship is its collection of traditional religious symbols, the verbal and the nonverbal, held in a stable tension. The liturgy gives us words to say and things to handle and do. It puts words on our lips to repeat, often before we actually perceive in our experience the presence of the ineffable mystery to which the language points. The liturgy forms us, intending, for example, that when the time comes, when life itself calls us to deny ourselves so that others might live, we will recognize "the time of our visitation."

Before 1963 we told ourselves with a measure of pride that it was the Latin liturgy itself which gave us a common Catholic identity.

"Go anywhere in the world," we said, "and the Mass will be the same everywhere." Now we realize that while we are a people bound by a common religious language, that language is not an ancient Mediterranean tongue. Rather, our common language is a stable set of symbols which refer us to the transcendent meanings that hold us together in Christ. Our task now is to claim these traditional symbols in the language of public life. Insofar as many of the symbols of public prayer are biblical at root, we have been helped in the work of shaping liturgical English by a five-hundred-year-old tradition of English Bible translations, beginning with the King James and the Douay-Rheims versions in the sixteenth and seventeenth centuries and in our own century with the Revised Standard Version, the Jerusalem Bible, and the New American Bible among others.

However, we must note that much of the prayer language of the Latin liturgical tradition did not rise directly from the Bible. Much liturgical Latin emerged from other sources, among them the metaphorical speaking of the bishops of Rome who presided over the prayer of that Church. These bishops—Leo, Gelasius, and Gregory—are credited with being forces in the development of the Latin liturgy. They effectively mediated the mystery of Christ by drawing directly on the idiom of Roman public life.

In post-Constantinian Rome, God was addressed not through the rhetoric of the biblical patriarchs, prophets, and apostles, but with the formal rhetoric of court ceremony: *clementissime Deus, omnipotens Deus*. So also, Christian burial rites were interpreted through Roman funerary institutions, with the result that our liturgical vocabulary and our liturgical architecture have been stabilized with the Roman cultural symbols of *refrigerium* and *martyrium*. In fact the whole complex of Christian rituals of public worship was itself interpreted by analogy with the imperial soldier's *sacramentum,* or public oathtaking.

Even the Eucharist liturgy got a Roman name: *munus*. The word's original field of meaning lay in the world of public office, public duty, public service, and public conferral of gifts. The more ancient memories of Jesus' meals with his disciples, of the eschatological banquet described by the prophets, of the table set by Lady Wisdom, were both enriched by and overshadowed by a new insight, namely, that the public assembling of Christians under the leadership of the bishop of Rome transcended and transposed all earlier traditions of public duty. The metaphor of Eucharist as *munus* brought religious insight to Roman citizens, and it has remained as a verbal symbol that has been handed on faithfully down to our generation. What do we do with *munus* in translations from liturgical Latin into an emerging liturgical English? abandon it? interpret its insight analogously with reference to our own public life? But is there an analogy? Translate the word literally and so aim simply to safeguard the symbol without preserving its insight? A brief look at the challenge of accurately translating the Roman post-Communion prayers into a slowly developing liturgical English illustrates the complexity of preserving the tradition of verbal liturgical symbols. All translation is already interpretation.

## Post-Communion Prayers and Traditional Liturgical Symbols

A Leonine scholar, David Holeton, shows that the words *mysterium, sacramentum,* and *munus* were virtually synonymous when they came from Pope Leo's pen or his lips. Used in a Eucharistic context, says Holeton, "*munus* is not bread and wine but the whole liturgical action whereby the saving mystery is commemorated and made present." The *mysterium* or *sacramentum* is not limited to the elements of bread and wine but rather includes the whole action. Later on, medieval theologians would lose the original insight because the liturgy itself had changed. The rite had broken down. The Church no longer focused on the importance of the public assembly of the local Church to perform its corporate public religious service under the leadership of its presiding officer. The clergy became accustomed to acting without an assembly. The nonverbal symbolic forms were shifting even while a stable Latin verbal form—Eucharist as *munus* or *mysterium* or *sacramentum*—was retained.

But the changed ritual activity eventually prompted a new insight. Priestly offering was understood to yield the sacramental gift of the sacred Body and Blood of Christ as a kind of distillate of the sacrificial act. The sacrament of the priest's sacrifice, the *munus,* or *mysterium,* was God's gift back to the Church after the priest had offered a gift to God on behalf of the (absent) Church.

Both of these understandings of *munus, mysterium, sacramentum*—as the whole action of the Church and as the elements for Communion—are part of the tradition of Latin liturgical symbols that have shaped our praying and our understanding. Both fields of meaning are available to the professional translators. Which meaning will be carried forward into our liturgical English? And does it really make any difference?

Looking at a single text of the prayer after Communion can illustrate the complexity of preserving the traditional verbal symbols in the process of translation. Is the prayer after Communion at the Easter Vigil to be prayed with reference to what has most immediately preceded it, the people's Communion, or with reference to all that has gone before it that evening: the lighting of the fire, the Paschal encomium, the narrating of the story of salvation, the baptisms of the elect, and the Eucharistic action of the whole Church culminating in the Eucharistic Communion of the whole assembly? When the presider invites the assembly to prayer in a brief formula that sums up that action, he asks, *"Spiritum nobis, Domine, tuae caritatis infunde,"* "Fill us to overflowing with the Spirit of your love." Then he describes our condition as a Church. We are a people *"quos sacramentis paschalibus satiasti."* A people satisfied, nourished—by what? The Latin says the *sacramentis paschalibus.* The emergent liturgical English says the Easter sacraments. What might the people be hearing and understanding by this language?

The Vigil participants have had their senses stimulated, their imaginations fed, their hearts moved to sentiments of gratitude and joy by the whole Vigil. It is not just Eucharistic Communion—even in both kinds—that has filled them to overflowing. Yet Catholic usage of the verbal symbol "sacrament" in our recent past has limited the range of our understanding. Catholics "know" sacraments number seven. The sacrament we have just received moments before is the Eucharist—in two kinds. Or the Easter sacraments celebrated at the Vigil might be as many as three—baptism, confirmation, and Eucharist. Just what does the English liturgical neologism "Easter sacraments" refer to?

The translators, alert to the Leonine origins of the original insight, have coined a term that is intended to point us to our comprehensive symbolic celebration of the redeeming paschal presence of God: in light and darkness, fire and water, silence and word, immersions and emersions, anointings and hand layings, as well as in eating and drinking. All these symbolic transactions which the local Church has been engaged in for a couple of hours are the *sacramentis paschalibus,* the Easter sacraments. The prayer after Communion just before the dismissal of the assembly refers to much more than what has occurred in the people's Communion. But what meaning will presiders and the community of the baptized find in the neologism? I would argue that if the Vigil is well celebrated the power of the whole ritual complex will begin to interpret the verbal symbol, for the Church will know by experience what has filled it to overflowing. But given a poor Vigil celebration or none at all, the phrase "Easter sacraments" will remain opaque in the praying.

## Summary and Conclusions

Because our English-language praying in liturgical assembly is inevitably bound to earlier metaphorical insights that shaped liturgical Latin, we will have to continue to probe for depth of meaning as we pray translated prayers. Well-celebrated, revitalized liturgical rites will move us some distance forward in regaining the original insights embedded in the symbols. Furthermore, the repetition of the translated metaphors can discipline us in the development of our own liturgical English. But this discipline can also block us from metaphorical flashes that are more authentically rooted in our own public tongue.

We are currently involved in circuitous movement, backward and forward, as a Church at prayer trying to connect simultaneously with several realities: our own faith, its traditional expression, and our experience. But neither the negotiation between verbal languages nor the relation between the verbal and nonverbal symbols are ends in themselves, games for linguists. Finding the right words for the liturgical assembly has a greater religious purpose: to correlate our public language with our perceptions of the mystery of Christ at work in our world and symbolically celebrated in our assemblies. We aim to move from experience, through silence, to common verbal symbol.

Our freedom to move rapidly in the crafting of liturgical English is restricted by the current reluctance of the Roman Congregations for Divine Worship and for the Doctrine of the Faith to encourage original texts not based on Latin ones. Viewed positively, the delay gives us time to understand the challenge we face. It also gives us time to discover the rhythms and cadences and syntax of a contemporary English appropriate to the task of speaking publicly of the ineffable.

The forthcoming English retranslation of the Roman Missal, projected for national conferences of bishops early in the decade of the

1990s, will illustrate how far we have come in twenty-five years in our search for a liturgical English that can release the power of the Latin verbal symbols. But the translation will also bear witness to the further challenge ahead for English-speaking Catholics: to speak in original ways of the abiding experience of salvation.

## Suggestions for Further Reading

Ramshaw, Gail. *Christ in Sacred Speech: The Meaning of Liturgical Language*. Philadelphia: Fortress, 1986. A readable study of the kinds of religious language and the rhetorical patterns the Church uses in its public worship and the ways these patterns shape faith.

Saliers, Don. "Symbol in Liturgy: Tracing the Hidden Languages," *Worship* 58, no. 1 (January 1984) 37–48. Considers in addition to the words of worship the hidden languages of time, place, sound and silence, the visible, tactile, and kinetic.

Schneiders, Sandra. *Women and the Word*. Mahwah, N.J.: Paulist, 1986. An essay-length exploration of the dominance of male imagery within the Bible, its impact on the tradition of biblical and liturgical spirituality, and its implications for the spiritual health of women and the spiritual well being of the Church.

# 6

---

# Contemplative Participation

St. Benedict begins the prologue to his *Rule* with an exhortation to the aspiring monastic: "Listen carefully . . . attend . . . with the ear of your heart." The admonition sets the theme for reflection on liturgical spirituality. We learn by heart the things we must do together in the liturgical assembly. We learn by heart in order to take to heart the saving mystery we celebrate. But learning by heart, listening with the ear of the heart, and taking to heart the mystery of Christ are the work of a lifetime, not a lesson to be mastered in a short course or a single day's participation.

How is life different for those who attend wholeheartedly to the liturgy we celebrate? Collecting verifiable data is not easy. But a story can suffice for what we lack in data to give us a common reference point. The center of the story is the medieval English bishop-martyr Thomas à Becket. The story suggests how liturgy made a difference in earlier ages. When we finish reflecting on it, we will need to ask what question the story poses for our time, so different from the world of medieval England.

## Liturgical Spirituality as Public Meaning

Becket's story has engaged the minds and imaginations of poets, dramatists, historians, and even cultural anthropologists. Fifteen years ago Becket's story attracted my attention as a liturgiologist who was beginning to question the connections between theological claims about the graced nature of liturgical action and empirical data about the actual impact of liturgy on human behavior. A colleague at the University of Kansas, a British Church historian, was giving introductory lectures to graduate students on using historical method for the study of religion. He chose as a case study what is a classical historiographer's challenge. How could the historian on the basis of available historical sources interpret what happened to Thomas à Becket the chancellor, political loyalist turned archbishop who unexpectedly turned against King Henry II, his former friend and longtime ally?

The historians line up all the documents: letters, eyewitness accounts, contemporary chronicles (see *The Becket Controversy*, Thomas Jones, ed. [New York: John Wiley, 1970]). But the pieces fail to produce an intelligible whole; something is missing. Historians continue to speculate: Was it political experience? a thirst for power? the convergence of external circumstances that caused Thomas the archbishop to defy Henry the king and through his defiance to change the course of Church-state relations in medieval England? Historians are most puzzled by the suddenness of the change in Thomas à Becket's behavior. Henry had bullied him, and Becket apparently thought himself cornered. He went into a profound depression and isolated himself from everyone for several days. Then he reappeared strong and confident, defiant of the king and a champion of the Church. The historiography lesson ends with the scholar's warning to the new graduate students. Sometimes the available data is inadequate to the researcher's challenge.

Months later with no further interest in Becket of my own, I was reading cultural anthropologist Victor Turner on the social power of public ritual. One essay in the collection focuses on Becket. Turner poses the same question I had met before: What had caused the turn of events, the change of heart in Becket that changed the course of medieval English history? Turner, British himself, turns to the same chronicles and letters, perhaps as to a familiar exercise from his own school days. But he also looks at the data with a new optic. One chronicler had observed that during his depressive seclusion in mid-October of 1170 Becket celebrated the Mass for the Feast of St. Stephen. Turner, ritual theorist, spots a flashing red light, a discrepancy in the liturgical calendar. Stephen's feast is December 26, and the archbishop Thomas certainly knew that. On the day in question, October

13, Thomas would appropriately have celebrated the Mass for Edward the Confessor, an English king and martyr who had died in 1066, a century earlier.

No record tells why Thomas flipped the pages in the Missal, only that he did so, turning from the Mass for the king and martyr Edward to the Mass for the protomartyr Stephen. Turner speculates. The record says Becket was depressed and that he sent more than once for his chaplain. That behavior suggests he was experiencing a religious crisis, confusion about what was being asked of him, uncertainty about the meaning of what was transpiring in his conflict with the king. Henry and Henry's allies were demanding nothing less than Becket's full submission to the king's demands for the Church. Turner's speculation begins by looking at the texts for the Mass, hardly erroneously chosen, so possibly deliberately chosen.

What words did this liturgical composition give Thomas à Becket to pray? Would these be a clue to the illumination Thomas received in his spiritual darkness?

The introit antiphon, *Sederunt principes, et adversum me loquebantur.* . . . (Princes sat and spoke against me: and the wicked persecuted me: help me, O Lord my God, for thy servant was employed in thy justifications), was followed by the verse "Blessed are the undefiled in the way, who walk in the law of the Lord." These verses from Ps 119 established a horizon within which Becket could interpret the terms of his struggle with the king. He was part of the recurrent conflict between temporal princes and the servant of God.

The collect of the day provided further insight into the way such a conflict for the servant's loyalties might be resolved: "Grant us, we beseech Thee, O Lord, to imitate what we revere, that we may learn to love even our enemies; for we celebrate the day of his birth to immortality who could even plead on behalf of his persecutors with thy Son our Lord Jesus Christ." This text invited Thomas to imagine a resolution in which he could resist the king's coercion through a strategy of nonretaliation. From this higher viewpoint he had no reason to try to mobilize an army to destroy his former friend Henry. The worst that might happen was that he would follow in the footsteps of the protomartyr Stephen. That very story of Stephen's martyrdom unfolded in the next liturgical text, the epistle (Acts 6, 7) that ends with the assurance that Stephen "fell asleep in the Lord."

The designated Gospel reading (Matt 23:34-39) might then have helped clarify his mission and its accompanying risks as archbishop of Canterbury: "Behold . . . Jesus said . . . [warning the authorities of his own day] I send to you prophets and wise men and scribes, and some of them you will put to death." Were he still listening with the ear of his heart, the Communion verse would have further illuminated Becket's search for meaning and direction: "I see the heavens opened, and Jesus standing on the right hand of the power of God: Lord Jesus, receive my spirit, and lay not this sin to their charge." The post-Communion prayer would then have sealed the whole meaning of this graced moment for the troubled archbishop: "May the mysteries which we have received help us, O Lord: and through the intercession of blessed Stephen thy martyr, may they confirm us in thine everlasting protection."

Victor Turner, ritual analyst and theorist on the role of public ritual in the social process, proposes this virtually neglected liturgical event as the turning point the historians could not find. Thomas à Becket's contemplative participation in liturgical prayer might well have effected the conversion to which everyone could bear witness later that same day. For the records agree. Becket left his solitude, and armed only with the cross he confidently strode into the royal court to advise the king that he would not submit.

But Turner gives his proposed interpretation another twist, for his interest is not simply in Becket's inner conversion but in the public effect of ritual activity. So Turner proposes that Becket's personal appropriation of the identity of faithful servant as potential martyr had a social consequence. It effectively controlled the king. Turner notes that in twelfth-century-England not only Thomas the archbishop but also Henry the king would be formed by the tradition of biblical-liturgical symbols. Becket, striding into the hall of the king armed only with the cross, scripted the transaction. At some preconscious level, the king would have known he had been offered the role of "the wicked princes of all the ages" who seek to destroy God's servants. Henry was checked. Historians agree again at this point. Henry did not order Becket's death. But Henry's cohorts, puzzled at the king's new-found caution in dealing with his enemy, became zealous on the king's behalf during the king's absence. In late December the king's men martyred the archbishop in his cathedral. Losing his life, Thomas won the victory for the Church a generation later.

What was going on here? Ritual theorists tell us that a ritual system gives believers a world to live in. A liturgical tradition's symbolic presentation of roles and relationships provides a script for living the human drama. Liturgical remembrance of Jesus carries the recurrent meaning—that there are two ways—the path of life and the path that leads to death. Liturgical remembrance of Jesus carries with it a warrant for believers that they can and must choose again and again which path they will walk.

The religious outlook and the way of life shaped by the liturgical celebration of the mystery of Christ is what we mean when we talk about biblical-liturgical spirituality. Liturgiologists tell us that Christian liturgical spirituality has a single dynamic. It celebrates one thing only: the paschal character of salvation. Pascha is the passing through death to life; the passing through suffering on the way to salvation. Pascha is the way of the martyr; it is the way of Christian marriage. It is the mystery of life itself: living toward death confident of resurrection. Life involves dying, risking death, pouring out one's own lifeblood to rescue others from the shadow of death. In the era in which Thomas à Becket and Henry II struggled this paschal message was publicly available and publicly agreed upon. People might switch roles—from God's good servants to the fiendish princes of the ages—but the available roles were known and the script familiar. Regular liturgical assembly reinforced what people already knew to be the truth about what life required. Pascha was the only publicly approved script for medieval European life. But we live in a different age.

## Liturgical Spirituality in a Pluralistic Culture

Ours is an age of pluralism. And cultural pluralism invovles multiple scripts for living. People and individuals are asked to choose from among them, or—failing choice—they are fated to select roles and relationships temporarily and randomly and to live with unintelligible incoherence. It might seem simple not to have to choose, but it is our fate as humans that we enjoy freedom with its accompanying risks.

For many centuries our classical natural law theory emphasized our similarity with animals. Natural law theory asserted that God had written into our natures whatever we needed for our good. Contemporary ethnologists, however, contrast our situation as humans with the situation of animal species, noting that we are genetically deprived because so little of what humans need to know for life is genetically coded. Yet if we are genetically poor, we are culturally rich. Cultures, as systems of symbols, provide fields of meaning or horizon within which we live with purpose. Religious revelations like the message of Sinai and the message of Jesus get translated by believers into religious cultures whose symbols, Scriptures, and institutions, interpreted within a faith community, provide a map for life.

Ancient Mediterranean and indigenous European cultures provided the cultural substratum within which evangelical faith took root, flourished through the birth of Christian culture, and gave order and purpose to public and personal life. Early on, ancient stories of the Celtic and Slavic peoples, their hopes and dreams, were taken up into the story of salvation in Christ as this story was mediated by the Catholic Church. But now, at the end of the twentieth century, all the cultural syntheses of the medieval past are crumbling. Christian cultural values struggle to make a way forward into a technological and post-technological world. Even the familiar culture of Roman Catholicism—the post-Tridentine synthesis of papal hegemony and clerical dominance in the local Churches—is collapsing. And the gospel of Jesus Christ, tied as it has been to these past syntheses, still venerable but weakened, is no longer given unquestioning credence as the good news of salvation.

We are being offered many alternate scripts for our public lives. Few of them are concerned about identifying roles as pointed as "God's good servants" and "the enemies of God." The new cultural scripts competing for our allegience are, nevertheless, stories about salvation and the way to walk to future glory. One such script for our mass society would cast most of us into the role of consumers, teaching us to set our hearts on things that perish. In this script for a consumer society, the managerial class, a new quasi-clerical elite determines (1) what will be profitable for them to set before us for our consumption and (2) how we might be motivated to desire it with all our hearts.

In the city in which I live, Washington, D.C., the consumer drama has taken a lethal turn for the young and the poor. Wanting to be conspicuous consumers immediately, children are being sucked up into the drug culture, which pays them ready money for helping dealers deliver goods on the street. Promised glory, they enter into lifelong bondage.

Another script for our public lives is militarism. It too offers a way to salvation in the form of protection from our brothers and sisters. But we must first be taught to view one another as enemies. The stage set for this script can be vast or narrow; the actors may be whole nations or only family members and neighbors. The script itself has many subplots, for there are many theaters of war. In this script life always comes for those who have the heart to deal death to others.

Recurrent themes in the newly available scripts for our public and personal lives are self-aggrandizement, self-inflation, self-promotion. These are in some sense forms of self-transcendence, for they intend to overcome group and personal limits. But they run at cross purposes to the paschal hope that authentic self-transcendence can come only from walking the path that Jesus trod, as did his disciples: Whoever would find their life must lose it, must lay it down, must be the least and the servant of all. No dominant culture past or present has ever completely internalized the paschal character of salvation. King Henry's loyalists, for example, considered destroying Becket the best way to save themselves. But in an age when the Christian story held public sway, such self-promotion at the expense of others was called sin, and the sinner was thought liable to judgment.

What can be done to maintain or promote the gospel message of salvation during this era of cultural crisis with its many competing visions of the path to life? Interestingly, Vatican II called for liturgical reform. Trusting the vision of leaders in the liturgical movement—Prosper Gueranger, Lambert Beauduin, Pius X and Pius XI, Virgil Michel—the bishops in council wagered that there was some connection between public liturgy and the reconstruction of the social order. Accordingly, what was to characterize this reform was "the full, conscious, and active participation of the laity."

Was the means chosen proportionate to the end desired? The jury will be out a long time deliberating that verdict. In fact, the judgment can only be eschatological, an assaying in the divine scales that balances grace and sin. Twenty-five years of evidence is hardly enough to weigh. But I would like to argue here, affirming the viewpoint of cultural theorists like Clifford Geertz and Victor Turner, that the intuitions of the current reform concerning the importance of lay liturgical participation are sound. I would only propose to refine the language describing the kind of lay participation that the moment requires.

## Contemplative Participation

The quality of lay liturgical participation the moment requires is contemplative, or mystical. I choose the term to press our understanding beyond what we have commonly understood by the call for full, conscious, and active participation. Contemplatives are attentive to presence. They are present to the mystery within which all life is lived. They are alert to and wait for manifestations of the sacred within the mundane. They see the traces of divine grace even in the shards of human brokenness and absurdity. They are awed by the evidence all around them that God slays and then gives life when all hope for life is gone.

Karl Rahner writes that "the devout Christian of the future will either be a 'mystic,' one who has 'experienced' something, or [the person] will cease to be anything at all." The liturgical reform, where it has been openly received, has enabled us to experience and to attend to the mystery of God as our own mystery. The mystery of the risen Christ is among us and within us; the Spirit of Jesus has been given to us. Whoever sees us glimpses God at work for the world's salvation. We ourselves as a people are the sacrament of that savlation.

Can anyone believe such claims? We can, but only if we experience ourselves as sacraments of salvation and celebrate what we experience. In an earlier age we looked solely to the Eucharistic species as evidence of divine presence. Or we may have looked to the ordained minister as *alter Christus*. Ordinarily, we set them apart and concentrated on them as the center of our celebration of the mystery of Christ. Now we recognize that our field of vision as Church was too narrow. It is all the baptized who are *alteri Christi*, other Christs, something Christian poets and mystics have known all along.

The rhetoric of *Sacrosanctum Concilium* calling for "full, conscious, and active participation" of the laity seemed initially to be calling for a quantitative increase in our ritual involvement. Laity were to participate through acclamations, responses, psalmody, antiphons, and songs on our tongues as well as through more frequent gestures, more diverse postures, and more regular Eucharistic Communion. To make us even more conscious we had commentators directing our attention now to this action, now to another. These were new experiences of bodily and mental engagement. Beyond this, laity were enjoined to take their rightful roles as liturgical ministers.

Sometimes in all this activity we have come dangerously close to wearying ourselves with ritual busyness. Yet subtly the ritual engagement—now become more familiar—is drawing the laity into mystery at levels beyond what we initially intended or understood to be possible. We are moving from self-conscious activity to contemplative participation, rooted in experience of the mystery of grace. Having internalized much of the new ritual behavior required of the laity in the *editio typica* of the Roman liturgical books, we are assuming our identity as the reformed and renewed Church of Jesus Christ. Let me speak concretely with the hope that you can summon up your own comparable experiences of liturgical participation—experiences that have moved from the ephemeral to the contemplative.

An assembly of five hundred Catholics spent three and a half hours engaged in the work of the Easter Vigil on a March Saturday night in the spring of 1989, twenty-five years after *Sacrosanctum Concilium*. On that March night, the Church of Holy Wisdom spent three and a half hours completing the liturgical initiation of one catechumen and receiving three baptized neighbors into full communion with the Catholic Church. Nobody seemed to falter or grow weary as the night went on. But in a contemplative distraction I mused that a pastor always used to do this work of baptism virtually alone in much less than an hour on a Saturday or Sunday afternoon. Yet we had cumulated more than seventeen hundred hours of Christian prayer on just this final night of the Triduum, exploring for ourselves and the newcomers the paschal character of salvation. Still musing, I was awed by the mystery within which I stood: working people, families with their children who took themselves seriously as the Church of Jesus Christ and who knew themselves to be responsible for the persistence and spread of the Christian faith in their otherwise very secular worlds.

These suburban parishioners had gone far beyond the surface demands of "full, conscious, and active participation" in liturgical rites toward unselfconscious conversion to the Christian mystery as the ultimate meaning of their own lives. Throughout the following Sundays of Easter they continued their work. One Sunday three young couples who were expecting the births of children came forward, and the whole assembly blessed them, parents and the unborn, with outstretched hands as the pastor spoke the word of blessing. Another Easter Sunday the whole assembly, with the associate pastor presiding, initiated an infant called Emily Caroline into the Church and initiated her bewildered young parents, her godparents, and their young daughter into new public identity in the Church. The assembled Church openly called them all to new maturity of faith and prayed that God would give the Holy Spirit of Jesus to them so that they would be suitable guardians and companions to Emily.

This community of the baptized acted with its own spiritual authority. So acting, it summoned and empowered others to act in the power of Christ. And I wondered, how can they be so confident in their liturgical acting and in their praying? How do they know they have this power within them? And the answer is of course that the liturgical rites, by giving the parishioners of Holy Wisdom responsible things to do in public worship, formed them to understand and to take their responsibility. They became, in the repetitive ritual doing over these past two decades, suitable agents of divine grace. I am witness to this mystery. They know with great simplicity who they are.

Could the pastor of Holy Wisdom accomplish these same symbolic celebrations of grace himself without the community of the baptized? Hardly, for the parishioners are themselves central to the symbolic manifestation of Christ's saving power. He might well do something else, as priests cut off from active assemblies of the baptized did for centuries. But if we believe our own dictum that sacraments cause grace by signifying, then what is set out in the ritual doing is integral to the meaning. Emily Caroline, her parents, and her godparents are more powerfully graced in the middle of the Sunday assembly than they are in isolation from it. So also a pastor's prayer is more powerful when the Church is there with him to say its own "Amen."

The simple awareness of their own identity as Church is spilling over for the people of Holy Wisdom into acts of social regeneration. A civic project was announced during this same springtime when they were forming new Christians. Help was needed to repair and rehabilitate neighborhood housing for the elderly and poor. A sizable number of parishioners from Holy Wisdom turned out donating their time, materials, and labor. The visit of a local Red Cross bloodmobile was announced; record numbers turned out to offer the gift of life.

Is neighborhood repair a suitable manifestation of liturgical spirituality? or blood donation for emergency use? But what would be more suitable? Does contemplative participation in the Eucharistic mystery of Christ draw Christians out of their closed worlds, sending them more confidently to live among nonbelievers? Does contemplative participation make them more pious or more generous? Those who lament the loss of mystery occasioned by the liturgical reform may well have lost hold of their once-preferred manifestation of Christ's presence in a too-narrow cult of the tabernacle and the altar. But there is another manifestation of the mystery now available to the world outside the sanctuary: the people of God being built up day by day into the body of Christ for the world's healing and reconciliation.

## Summary and Conclusion

There is no longer a medieval Christian culture. Nor is there a post-Tridentine culture of Roman Catholicism to sustain the Church's claim that it can show the world the way to salvation. The many cultural offers of salvation through self-promotion available at the end of the twentieth century make the demanding Christian message even less attractive as good news. Those of us who continue to believe in the paschal mystery as the only true offer of salvation must embody the mystery, incarnate it again for a skeptical world. To do so, we must always struggle to overcome our own faintheartedness and our own readiness to doubt. Corporate public ritual, say the theorists, gives participants an experience of ultimate mystery. Contemplative participation in the paschal mystery of Christ, say the people of Holy Wisdom, makes possible the appropriation of the identity the rites offer. Augustine instructed the Church long ago: "Become who you are, the Body of Christ." That, in sum, is the effect of liturgical spirituality.

## Suggestions for Further Reading

Collins, Mary. "Who Are the Hearers of the Word," *Worship: Renewal to Practice*. Washington: The Pastoral Press, 1987. A reflection on the many competing symbol systems operating in our pluralistic culture that vie for people's attention and allegiance.

Dillard, Annie. *Holy the Firm*. New York: Harper & Row, 1977.

Franklin, R. W. "Gueranger: A View on the Centenary of His Death," *Worship* 49, no. 6 (June–July 1975) 318–28. An assessment of the relationship between public worship and the revitalization of community as understood by the leader of the nineteenth century liturgical movement.

Turner, Victor. "Religious Paradigms and Political Action: Thomas Becket at the Council of Northampton," *Dramas, Fields, and Metaphors: Symbolic Action in Human Society*. Ithaca, N.Y., and London: Cornell University Press, 1974.

# Epilogue

"A blur of romance clings to our notions of 'publicans,' 'sinners,' 'the poor,' 'the people in the market place,' 'our neighbors,' as though of course God should reveal himself, if at all, to these simple people, these Sunday school watercolor pictures who are so purely themselves in their tattered robes, who are single in themselves, while we now are various, complex, and full at heart. We are busy. So, I see now, were they. Who shall ascend into the hill of the Lord? or who shall stand in his holy place? There is no one but us. There is no one to send, nor a clean hand, nor a pure heart on the face of the earth, nor in the earth, but only us, a generation comforting ourselves with the notion that we have come at an awkward time, that our innocent fathers are all dead—as if innocence had ever been—and our children busy and troubled, and we ourselves unfit, not yet ready, having each of us chosen wrongly, made a false start, failed, yielded to impulse and the tangled comfort of pleasures, and grown exhausted, unable to seek the thread, weak, and involved. But there is no one but us. There never has been. There have been generations which remembered, and generations which forgot; there has never been a generation of whole men and women who lived well for even one day. Yet some have imagined well, with honesty and art, the detail of such a life, and have described it with such grace, that we mistake vision for history, dream for description, and fancy that life has devolved. So. You learn this studying any history at all, especially the lives of artists and visionaries; you learn it from Emerson, who noticed that the meanness of our days is itself worth our thought; and you learn it, fitful in your pew, at church."

Annie Dillard
*Holy the Firm* *

*Excerpt from *Holy the Firm* (New York: Harper & Row, Publishers, Inc., 1977). Copyright © 1977 by Annie Dillard.